m

THE WARRIOR'S HONOR

Scar Tissue

Blood and Belonging: Journeys into the New Nationalism

The Russian Album

The Needs of Strangers

A Just Measure of Pain

Ethnic War and the

THE
WARRIOR'S
HONOR

Modern Conscience

Michael Ignatieff

METROPOLITAN BOOKS

HENRY HOLT AND COMPANY   NEW YORK

Metropolitan Books
Henry Holt and Company, Inc.
Publishers since 1866
115 West 18th Street
New York, New York 10011

Portions of early versions of these essays appeared in different form in the following:
"Is Nothing Sacred? The Ethics of Television" appeared in *Daedalus,* Fall 1985.
Part of "The Narcissism of Minor Difference" appeared as "Nationalism and
Toleration" in Richard Caplan and John Feffer (eds.), *Europe's New Nationalism*
(New York, 1996). "The Seductiveness of Moral Disgust" appeared in *Social
Research,* vol. 62, no. 1, Spring 1995; the portion of the text devoted to the
secretary-general's trip through Africa in July 1995 appeared in *The New Yorker,*
August 10, 1995. Part of "The Warrior's Honor" appeared as "Unarmed Warriors"
in *The New Yorker,* March 24, 1997. "The Nightmare from Which We Are Trying
to Awake" was delivered as the Joyce Lecture, Dublin, June 1995; a part of the text
also appeared as "Articles of Faith" in *Index on Censorship,* vol. 25, no. 5, 1996.

Library of Congress Cataloging-in-Publication Data
Ignatieff, Michael.
The warrior's honor : ethnic war and the modern conscience /
Michael Ignatieff. — 1st American ed.
p.   cm.
Includes bibliographical references and index.
ISBN 0-8050-5518-5 (hc : alk. paper)
1. Ethnic relations.   2. Social conflict.   3. Social justice.
4. Mass media and ethnic relations.   5. Humanitarian assistance.
I. Title.
GN496.I55   1998
305.8—dc21   97-28245

Henry Holt books are available for special promotions and premiums.
For details contact: Director, Special Markets.

First American Edition 1998

Designed by Kate Nichols

Printed in the United States of America
All first editions are printed on acid-free paper. ∞
1   2   3   4   5   6   7   8   9   10

For Suzannu

Contents

THE WARRIOR'S HONOR

Introduction

BETWEEN 1993 AND 1997, I traveled through the landscapes
of modern ethnic war: to Serbia, Croatia, and Bosnia; to Rwanda,
Burundi, Angola; and to Afghanistan. I saw the ruins of Vukovar,
Huambo, and Kabul; the bodies in the church at Nyarubuye; and
the orphans of Mazar al Sharif. At the checkpoints I met the new
warriors: the barefoot boys with Kalashnikovs, the paramilitaries
in wraparound sunglasses, the turbaned zealots of the Taliban
who checked their prayer mats next to their guns.

I happened to be making my journeys just after a new tide of
interventionist internationalism had swelled during the Gulf War
and before it ebbed away in Bosnia. I wanted to find out what
mixture of moral solidarity and hubris led Western nations to
embark on this brief adventure in putting the world to rights.
What impulses led us to supervise elections in Cambodia, try
to protect the Kurds from Saddam, send U.N. troops to Bosnia,

restore democracy to Haiti, bring the warriors to the table in Angola? And what, if anything, still connects the zones of safety where I and most readers of this book are likely to live and the zones of danger where ethnic struggle has become a way of life?

In an earlier book, *The Needs of Strangers,* I was concerned with moral obligation between strangers in domestic contexts, within nation states. My concern here is with moral obligation beyond our tribe, beyond our nation, family, intimate network. *The Warrior's Honor* is about that impulse we all feel to "do something" when we see some terrible report on television from Bosnia or Rwanda or Afghanistan. Why exactly do some of us feel that these strangers are our responsibility? What scripts and narratives of involvement get some of us to commit ourselves to people we had no connection to until some chance encounter with televised images of atrocity galvanized us into action?

In the nineteenth century, imperial interest bound the two worlds together: ivory, gold, and copper sent the imperial agents into the heart of darkness. During the fifty years of the Cold War, the presence of one superpower's agents, spies, or mercenaries in any particular ethnic war guaranteed the presence of the other on the opposing side. Now there is no narrative of imperial rivalry or ideological struggle that compels the zones of safety to make the zones of danger their business. What is left is a narrative of compassion, and it is this connection—inconstant and ambiguous—that is my subject.

It isn't obvious why strangers in peril halfway across the world *should* be our business. For most of human history, the boundaries of our moral universe were the borders of tribe, language, religion, or nation. The idea that we might have obligations to human beings beyond our borders simply because we belong to the same species is a recent invention, the result of our awakening to the shame of having done so little to help the millions of strangers who died in this century's experiments in terror and extermination. Nothing good has come of these experiments except perhaps the consciousness that we are all Shakespeare's "thing itself": unaccommodated man, the poor, bare forked animal. It is "the thing itself" that has become the subject—and the rationale —for the modern universal human rights culture.

The essays that follow explore the moral connections that this new culture enables us to create. Some of the essays are about the Westerners who make the misery of strangers their business: the outrage and ideals that spur their involvement, the moral complexities that follow engagement, and the cycle of disillusion that often accompanies burnout and disengagement. Such involvement is a crucial new feature of the modern moral imagination. In the nineteenth century, these people would have been diplomats, missionaries, and commanders of imperial hill stations. Now they are aid workers, reporters, lawyers for war crimes tribunals, human rights observers, all working in the name of an impalpable moral ideal: that the problems of other people, no matter how far away, are of concern to us all. But almost everyone who tries to live by this ideal has a bad conscience: no one is quite sure whether our engagement makes things better or worse; no one is quite sure how far our engagement should extend; no one is quite sure how deep our commitments really are—they are mediated by television, after all, and our engagement may be intense but shallow. Conrad's fable of moral disgust—*Heart of Darkness*—continues to have a disturbing pertinence.

My second major theme is: Having gotten involved, what are we faced with? What is happening to make the world seem so dangerous and chaotic? Who are the new architects of postmodern war, the paramilitaries, guerrillas, militias, and warlords who are tearing up the failed states of the 1990s? War used to be fought by soldiers; it is now fought by irregulars. This may be one reason why postmodern war is so savage, why war crimes and atrocities are now integral to the very prosecution of war.

There is a moral disconnection between these new war makers and the liberal interventionists who represent our moral stakes. We in the West start from a universalist ethic based on ideas of human rights; they start from particularist ethics that define the tribe, the nation, or ethnicity as the limit of legitimate moral concern. What many agencies, including the Red Cross, have discovered is that human rights have little or no purchase on this world of war. Far better to appeal to these fighters as warriors than as human beings, for warriors have codes of honor; human beings—qua human beings—have none. Even then, what is a warrior's honor to a destitute orphan with a Kalashnikov or to some ethnic irregular who survives by pillage and predation? As states disintegrate, so do armies and chains of command, and, with them, the indigenous warrior codes that sometimes keep war this side of bestiality. This is the desperate context in which international aid workers struggle to find moral vernaculars and strategies of assistance to prevent ethnic war from degenerating into genocide.

A further theme of this book is the impact of ethnic war abroad on our thinking about ethnic accommodation at home. The savagery of these wars has made misanthropy a seductive temptation. It is easy to think of ethnic war as an atavistic eruption of the incorrigible tribalism lurking in all of us and as proof that it is hopeless to expect different races and ethnic groups to live together. Ever since Conrad's *Heart of Darkness,* travelers returning from the zones of danger have used their experiences to castigate the liberal illusions of those who live in the zones of safety.

In fact, though, there is nothing in our natures that makes ethnic or racial conflict unavoidable. The idea that different races and ethnic groups can coexist in peace and even goodwill is not a hopeless illusion. Even the long-standing, apparently adamantine antipathies of the ethnic war zones turn out, on closer examination, to be expressions of fear created by the collapse or absence of institutions that enable individuals to form civic identities strong enough to counteract their ethnic allegiances. When individuals live in stable states—even poor ones—they do not need to rush to the protection of the group. It is the disintegration of states, and the Hobbesian fear that results, that produces ethnic fragmentation and war.

The final theme I address is memory and moral healing: How do societies come awake from war and savagery? How do they put the unbearable past behind them? Again, liberal interventionists go into these zones with pieties about the healing virtues of truth and the moral necessity of justice when sometimes what these societies need is forgetting. *We* begin with the psychoanalytic virtues of truth; *they* have learned the necessity of repression. All truth is good, says the African proverb, but is all truth good to say? This is the dilemma that faces war crimes tribunals and truth commissions. There are limits to the healing that outsiders can bring. Ethnic war remains a family quarrel, a duel to the death between brothers that can only be resolved within the family, and only when fear no longer rules.

There is no reason to despair. For every society like Afghanistan mired in ethnic conflict, there is a South Africa making its arduous journey back from the abyss. As soon as the world pronounces some part of the world beyond hope—Central Africa, for example—leaders appear who seem capable of forging the strong and legitimate states these regions need if they are to lift themselves out of the pit of war. For every failed intervention like

Somalia there is an Angola, where some hope remains that a durable peace can be brokered. Just when the world appears to be letting war criminals off the hook, some are brought to justice and the cycle of impunity is broken.

The world is not becoming more chaotic or violent, although our failure to understand and act makes it seem so. Nor has the world become more callous. Weak as the narrative of compassion and moral commitment may be, it is infinitely stronger than it was only fifty years ago. We are scarcely aware of the extent to which our moral imagination has been transformed since 1945 by the growth of a language and practice of moral universalism, expressed above all in a shared human rights culture. Television in its turn makes it harder to sustain indifference or ignorance. Finally, the army of aid workers and activists who mediate between the zones of our world continues to grow in strength and influence. They remain our moral alibi, but they are also the means through which deeper and more permanent commitments can be made in the future. There is nothing in the emergence of this global conscience that gives us reason to be complacent. But there is also nothing that justifies disillusion.

Is Nothing Sacred?
The Ethics of Television

I

THE BRITISH NURSE was picking her way through the mass of women and children squatting in the dust at the entrance to the field hospital of the refugee camp at Korem in Ethiopia. She was selecting which children could still be helped. She was choosing who would live and who would die. A television crew trailed behind her, moving its way among the starving. A television reporter approached with a mike and asked her how she felt about what she was doing. It was not a question she felt capable of answering. The look she gave the camera came from very far away.

IT IS IN SCENES like this one, with questions like this, that television confronts consciences of the West with suffering in the zones of famine and ethnic war. Through its news broadcasts and spectaculars like "Live Aid," television has become the privileged medium through which moral relations between strangers are mediated in the modern world. Yet the effects of televisual images and the rules and conventions of electronic news-gathering on such moral relations are rarely examined. At first sight, the moral relations created by these images could be interpreted in radically different ways, either as an instance of the promiscuous voyeurism a visual culture makes possible or as a hopeful example of the internationalization of conscience. The difficulty, of course, is that both of these opposing interpretations may be true. Let us take each in turn.

There is little doubt, first of all, that the television coverage of famine and war has had a remarkable impact upon Western charity. In Britain alone, more than sixty million pounds was donated to famine relief agencies in the year after the Ethiopian footage was first shown in October 1984. For the first time since Biafra, governments throughout Europe found themselves under continuous public pressure on a development issue. Many facts known but relegated to the realm of the taken-for-granted—the tons of surplus grain produced by the European Union's agricultural policy—suddenly became a public scandal when juxtaposed with the images of starvation. TV brought public pressure to bear upon the bureaucratic inertia—and ideological excuses—that had allowed a long-predicted food crisis to become a disaster. Television helped to forge a direct relation of people to people that cut through bilateral governmental mediations. For a brief moment, it created a new kind of electronic internationalism linking the consciences of the rich and the needs of the poor. As a medium, television dramatically reduced the lag-time between pressure and action, between need and response. Without it, thousands more victims of starvation and war would have died, as they have died unseen and unlamented until the advent of television.

Yet if this is the case for television's good conscience, there are other more troubling aspects to the gaze it cast on disaster. There is the accusation that TV news ignores food shortages until they acquire epic visual appeal, and there is the suspicion that the story drops out of the nightly bulletins when the focus upon horror shifts elsewhere in the world. The medium's gaze is brief, intense, and promiscuous. The shelf life of the moral causes it makes its own is brutally short. Other disquieting aspects of the televisual gaze are brought into focus by the reporter's question to the nurse: How do you feel? The question may have come out of a desire to reach out across the distance the reporter knew separated her from those watching in their living rooms. It may also have come out of a need to fill the silence of those starving at his feet. But the question served only to make plain the chasm that empathy—"suffering with"—cannot hope to cross. The question laid bare the interstellar moral distances that a culture of visual images conjures away with its cruel mime of immediacy.

On the one hand, television has contributed to the breakdown of the barriers of citizenship, religion, race, and geography that once divided our moral space into those we were responsible for and those who were beyond our ken. On the other hand, it makes us voyeurs of the suffering of others, tourists amid their landscapes of anguish. It brings us face-to-face with their fate, while obscuring the distances—social, economic, moral—that lie between us. It is this tangle of contradictory, mutually canceling, effects that I want to try to unravel.

II

TELEVISION IMAGES cannot assert anything; they can only instantiate something. Images of human suffering do not assert their own meaning; they can only instantiate a moral claim if those who watch understand themselves to be potentially under obligation to those they see. Behind the seemingly natural mechanics of empathy at work in viewers' response to these images lies a history by which their consciences were formed to respond as they do. It is the history by which Europeans gradually came to believe in a myth of human universality—the simple idea that race, religion, sex, citizenship, or legal status do not justify unequal treatment; or, more positively, that human needs and pain are universally the same, and that we may be obliged to help those to whom we are unrelated by birth or citizenship, race or geographic proximity.

The Christian promise of the universality of salvation was the first ethical claim to confront the classical partition of humanity into citizens and slaves, and the medieval common law built this idea of the identity of all human subjects into the basis of European legal systems. With the Reformation, the human universality premised on the unity of Christendom had to be thought anew for a world divided into warring confessions. The jurisprudence developed by early modern natural law theorists sought to provide a universal natural law for a world of sharply conflicting laws and ethics. Natural law was centrally concerned with defining the rights of those strangers—prisoners of war, survivors of wrecks—who happened to fall from one jurisdiction into another, or who fell between them, and who thus stood in defenseless dependence on a culture of obligation between themselves and their captors or rescuers. Much of this struggle to define and defend the rights of a universal subject went on against a somber backdrop of religious war.

From the pens of Montaigne, Bayle, Locke, and many others who were disgusted by the ways in which partial human identities—religion, nation, region—were used to justify the slaughter of other human beings, there emerged the modern doctrine of toleration. Its central claim, as Judith Shklar and others have pointed out, was to deny that sins against God—blasphemy, heresy, disobedience—justified sins against men. No higher law could justify the nonjudicial taking of human life. The exponents of the doctrine of toleration also insisted that, given the shared human ignorance about the ultimate metaphysical foundations of the world, all human creatures had an equal right to construe those foundations as best they could, provided they did no harm to the property and lives of others. The philosophical ground for civil peace among confessional communities within and between states, the seventeenth-century philosophers argued, was a shared adherence to the idea of natural human identity and equality.

All of this applied, of course, only to white males within the European world, but its application to the nonwhite peoples encountered on the frontier of the European penetration of North and South America was only too apparent to sixteenth-century figures like the essayist Montaigne and the Spanish missionary Las Casas. If their pens were unable to halt or delay the decimation that accompanied European imperialism, they helped to create the sense of guilt that is as much at the heart of the imperialist story as conquest itself. If European imperialism divided the world into "us" and "them," white and black, Christian and heathen, civilized and savage, there was always present in the European conscience a Christian and jurisprudential universalism that rejected this particularist definition of human obligations. We are still living out the history of conscience that began with the first European voyages of discovery, but surely one of the moments when the universalist definition of human identity won an irreversible victory over the particularist was the successful campaign against the slave trade, and then against slavery itself, from 1780 to 1850. Certainly, the intentions at work in these campaigns were not exclusively high-minded: the costs of slavery, the relative inefficiency of slaves compared to free labor, also counted in the squaring of the pocketbook and the conscience. Indeed, this whole story cannot be written as a progressive unfolding of moral enlightenment, but rather as a struggle to reconcile universalist moral impulses with their often uncomfortable consequences.

Some of these consequences were brought into sharp focus by the issue of famine. From the time of the early church fathers, the question of whether the duty to relieve the needs of the poor was a compulsory obligation or a voluntary one was central in the debate about the public ethics of a Christian person. If the obligation was one of justice, the needs of the poor might be said to give them a right to the property of the rich. Church fathers like Aquinas were concerned that this right would unsettle the fixed entitlement to property that was the basis of social order itself. On the other hand, if the poor had no rights and had to depend on charity alone, many of them were bound to starve in times of famine. The history of Christian ethics revolved around this debate between the rights of property and the claims of the poor in time of famine. In practice, the claims of ethical universalism came to be strongly limited in Christian teaching and then in European natural law by the injunction that a rich man had a merely voluntary charitable obligation to strangers in need. In more general terms, a descending order of moral impingement came into place: the claims of kith and kin first, then neighbors, co-religionists, co-citizens, and only at the very end, the indeterminate stranger. To this day, the claim of the stranger—the victim on the TV screen—is the furthest planet in the solar system of our moral obligations. The claim that we should help those "closer to home" will always be persuasive. Whether or not it is right to be so persuaded is another matter. There is thus a great deal of moral confusion in the supposed natural outflow of charitable empathy overseas. And it reflects a long-standing conflict between the conscience of ethical universalism and the demands of a private property system, and between the known subject of need and the stranger at the gate.

Faced with this contradiction, the Marxist tradition has always regarded bourgeois moral universalism as a veil of ideological deception. Marxists have also argued that the doctrine of the natural inviolability of all individuals as rights-bearing creatures could become a reality only in societies that do away with capitalist and imperialist social relations. The history of Marxist sarcasm toward bourgeois universalism would give special mention to Maurice Merleau-Ponty's *Humanism and Terror*, written as a reply to liberal and socialist critiques of the show trials of Stalin. The humanist critique of Soviet political violence, Merleau-Ponty argued, was a hypocritical attempt to deny the violence constitutive of bourgeois rule itself, as well as an attempt to delegitimize a revolution's necessary means of self-defense. The pity of bourgeois humanism, Merleau-Ponty argued, refused to understand that violence has been the motor of progress from the rise of the bourgeoisie to the triumph of the Soviet revolution.

Roland Barthes's essay on the photographic exhibit "The Family of Man" belongs to this postwar French Marxist counterattack on bourgeois humanism, and extended Merleau-Ponty's line of argument into the realm of aesthetics. The exhibition's celebration of man's natural human identity—his membership in "the family of man"—Barthes argued, reduced real historical men and women to the inconsequential sameness of their zoological identity. In doing so, the images sought to wrap essential elements of human experience—work, play, suffering, and grief—in an aura of eternal inevitability, and thus to remove suffering and oppression from the ambit of human agency.

If we follow this Marxist critique of bourgeois cant, the shame of televised images of horror would lie not in what they show, but in what they suppress. The culture of the visual image, so a Marxist would argue, moralized the relation between viewer and sufferer as an eternal moment of empathy outside history. Television presents economic and political relations as human relations, and asserts a connection between the Western conscience and the needs of the strangers of the Third World as inhering in human nature itself, beneath the history of exploitation that links the West to its neocolonial hinterland. In this view, the charity unleashed by empathy is a form of forgetting, the reproduction of amnesia about the responsibility of the West for the causes of famine and war.

It is doubtless true that the mechanisms of pity are a complex mixture of forgetting and condescension, and that heightened self-regard is an integral part of the glow of moral empathy with the suffering of others. Yet television's—and our own—encounter with these images is considerably more ambivalent than such an analysis would suggest. While it is easy to argue that a culture of the visual image favors the icons of suffering over the tomes of analysis, it simply has not suppressed analysis of its causes. Every structural feature of the Ethiopian famine—the arms race in the Horn of Africa, the injustices of the world commodity price system, the failure of Western development agencies to invest sufficiently in soil reclamation, land reform, and resettlement projects, the grotesque fact that local rulers fight their civil wars instead of attending to the needs of their peoples—all these have been documented on television. If viewers take it for granted that the starving are, to some degree, their business, the reason is that the pictures have been preceded by more than a decade of documentaries on Third World development, which, while tending to favor the ideology of Robert McNamara at the expense of Franz Fanon, have at least made plain some of the structures of neocolonial economic and political dependency. Current-affairs television did not create this new culture of understanding between First and Third Worlds that mediates the flow of empathy between viewer and sufferer, but it has played an honest and sometimes honorable part in building an inchoate popular understanding of development issues in Western public opinion. If television is bourgeois ideology, then the least we have to say is that bourgeois ideology in relation to the Third World—is a deeply complex mixture of willed amnesia, guilty conscience, moralizing self-regard, and real understanding. Television does not suppress this ambivalence; it faithfully reproduces it in all its confusion.

The myth of human identity, that vision of common human needs and common human pain that binds viewer and sufferer together, is itself fraught with ambiguity. White viewers who mail checks on behalf of black victims at the other side of the globe may combine their generosity with very different behavior toward blacks nearer home. One of empathy's pleasures is to forget one's moral inconsistencies. Yet the claim that moral empathy at this distance is nothing more than self-deceiving myth relies tacitly on a moral myth of its own: that full "suffering with," based on commonality of experience, is possible only among persons who share the same social identity, for example, the same class. Class identity, however, is no less mythic, no less imagined, than universal human brotherhood. The ethics that derive from it must divide the world into us and them, friends and enemies.

Moral internationalism based on class solidarity has had its hours of glory—the International Brigade in Spain, for example—but also its hours of ignominy. When the Soviet tanks rolled into Hungary and Czechoslovakia, the troops were told they were marching to the aid of their comrades against the common class enemy. "Weeding out the class enemy" has been the moral *mot d'ordre* for the atrocities committed by the Soviet and partisan armies after World War II, not to mention in the rice paddies of Kampuchea. If the fragile internationalism of the myth of human brotherhood has returned as a moral force in the modern world, it is because partial human solidarities—those of religion, ethnicity, and class—have dishonored themselves by the slaughter committed in their name.

In the twentieth century, however, this myth has a more somber moral hue than such nineteenth-century antecedents as the evangelical campaigns against the slave trade and Gladstone's campaign against the Bulgarian atrocities. Nineteenth-century "bourgeois humanism" drew its inspiration from the political economy of free trade—with its vision of a world of peoples brought together in a world market; from a doctrine of progress that understood the spread of the British imperium as an instance of the march of the human mind, and that conceived of human universality in terms of bringing the lesser breeds within the law of civilization.

In the twentieth century, the idea of human universality rests less on hope than on fear, less on optimism about the human capacity for good than on dread of human capacity for evil, less on a vision of man as maker of his history than of man the wolf toward his own kind. The way stations on the road to this new internationalism were Armenia, Verdun, the Russian front, Auschwitz, Hiroshima, Vietnam, Cambodia, Lebanon, Rwanda, and Bosnia. A century of total war has made victims of us all, civilians and military, men, women, and children alike. We no longer live in a time when violence is distributed—and pity and compassion too—along the lines of tribe, race, religion, or nation. If new technology has created a new form of war and a new crime—genocide—we have also witnessed the creation of a new kind of victimhood. War and genocide have overturned the moral boundary-markers of citizenship, race, and class that used to allocate responsibility for the relief of the suffering. If we take it for granted now that suffering strangers are our responsibility, it is because a century of total destruction has made us ashamed of that cantonment of moral responsibilities by nation, religion, or region that resulted in the abandonment of the Jews. Modern moral universalism is built upon the experience of a new kind of crime: the crime against humanity.

Famine and ethnic war pulverize huge numbers of different individuals into exactly equal units of pure humanity. In the camps that dotted northeastern Europe over fifty years ago, peasants from Poland, bankers from Hamburg, Gypsies from Romania, shopkeepers from Riga—each with a separate social identity and a different kind of relation to their oppressor—were placed on the anvil of suffering and hammered into sameness and then into oblivion. In the Ethiopian camps, highland Christians, lowland Muslims, Eritreans, Tigreans, Afars, and Somalis were reworked on the anvil of suffering into the sameness of victimhood. In this process of fission, each individual is severed from the social relations that, in normal times, would have saved their lives. Each individual in the Ethiopian camps was a son, a daughter, a father, a mother, a tribesman, a citizen, a believer, a neighbor. But none of these social relations will sustain an appeal for help in a time of distress. Famine, like genocide, destroys the capillary system of social relations that sustains each individual's system of entitlements. In so doing, genocide and famine create a new human subject—the pure victim stripped of social identity, and thus bereft of the specific moral audience that would in normal times be there to hear his cry. The family, the tribe, the faith, the nation no longer exist as a moral audience for these people. If they are to be saved at all, they must put their faith in that most fearful of dependency relations: the charity of strangers.

Human brotherhood in these conditions, therefore, can be understood as a residual moral system of obligations among strangers that comes into force when all other social relations capable of saving a person have been destroyed. In this sense, human brotherhood is a myth made actual and concrete by the history of twentieth-century horror: it is a myth with a history, a necessity only history can give. It is a moral truism, put to the test in the twentieth century on a scale never before imagined, that there is no such thing as love of the human race, only love of this person or that, in this time and place. Obligations, it is always said, are social, contextual, relational, and historical. But what, then, is to be done for those whose social and historical relations have been utterly pulverized? Human life is now confronted with a range of new conditions—continent-wide famines, ecological catastrophe, and genocide—that constitute victims who have no social relations capable of mobilizing their salvation, and who, as a result, make an ethic of universal moral obligation among strangers a necessity for the future of life on the planet. Doubtless such an ethic of obligation will always have a secondary claim on our moral will, subsidiary to the attentions we lavish on a brother, a sister, a fellow citizen, a cobeliever, or a coworker. But without this weak and inconstant ethic, this impersonal commitment to strangers, the universal victim will find no one beyond the wire to feed him. It is this weak moral language, and the new experience of universal victimhood it is trying to address, of which television has become the privileged modern medium.

III

TELEVISION IS ALSO the instrument of a new kind of politics. Since 1945, affluence and idealism have made possible the emergence of a host of nongovernmental private charities and pressure groups—Amnesty International, Care, Save the Children, Christian Aid, Oxfam, Médicins sans Frontières, and others—that use television as a central part of their campaigns to mobilize conscience and money on behalf of endangered humans and their habitats around the world. It is a politics that takes the world rather than the nation as its political space and that takes the human species itself rather than specific citizenship, racial, religious, or ethnic groups as its object. It is a "species politics" striving to save the human species from itself, as Greenpeace and World Wildlife are striving to protect natural and animal species from the predator man. These organizations seek to circumvent the bilateral governmental relations between peoples and institute direct political contacts between, for example, Amnesty sponsors and particular prisoners, or American families and Latin American foster children, or field service volunteers and their peasant clients. It is a politics that has tried to construct a world public opinion to keep watch over the rights of those who lack the means to protect themselves. Using the medium of television, many of these international organizations have managed to force governments to pay some degree of attention to the public-relations costs of their exercises in domestic repression.

These organizations also try to raise these costs wherever they can, by persuading Western nations to tie loan agreements, arms contracts, and development packages to certain standards of behavior in the field of human rights. As a result, what happens in the jails of Kigali, Kabul, Beijing, and Johannesburg has become the business of television viewers across the world. At a time when the politics of nation-states, party ideology, and civic activism alike show signs of exhaustion, disillusion, and impasse, this new politics has shown itself a robust mobilizer of commitment and money. Its popularity owes much to the fact that it is an antipolitics, rejecting all the arguments that political ideologists devise to justify harm done to human beings. It is also an antipolitics in its refusal to differentiate among victims. Amnesty International, for example, refuses to differentiate between right-wing or left-wing political prisoners, between torture conducted in the name of socialist revolution or torture conducted in the name of American-style freedom.

Television is particularly well suited to certain features of this kind of politics, able as it is to bring political intentions and their consequences face-to-face with each other: with one flick of an editing switch, television can point out the gulf of abstraction that separates the politician's speech about the defense of freedom from the butchered bodies in the jungle. At its best, television's morality is the morality of the war correspondent, the veteran who has heard all the recurring justifications for human cruelty advanced by the Left and the Right, and who learns in the end to pay attention only to the victims. Don McCullin, the British war photographer, voiced this ethic in his introduction to a collection of some of his photographs of Biafra, Bangladesh, and Vietnam:

> But what are my politics? I certainly take the side of the underprivileged. I could never say I was politically neutral.

But whether I'm of the Right or the Left—I can't say. I feel I'm trapped by my background, my inability to retain facts, and my utter bewilderment when faced by political theory: I'm so defeated by it I don't even vote. I've tried to be a witness, an independent spectator, with the result that I can't get beyond the facts of what I've seen. I've experienced too much suffering. I feel, in my guts, at one with the victims. And I find there's integrity in that stance.

Television's good conscience could be described in much the same terms: to pay attention to the victims, rather than the pieties of political rhetoric; to refuse to make a distinction between good corpses and bad ones (though this was notoriously not the case in American coverage of Vietnam); and to be a witness, a bearer of bad tidings to the watching conscience of the world. This is the moral internationalism of the 1980s and 1990s, and it is a weary world away from the internationalism of the 1960s. If someone had said in 1967 that he refused to distinguish between the human rights violations of the Americans and the North Vietnamese, he would have been set upon by Right and Left in equal measure. But now that a North Vietnamese victory has been followed with further wars of aggrandizement, a moral position that assesses ideologies by the victims they leave behind has gained the right to be heard above the righteous din.

There are fashions in morals as there are fashions in clothes. Television followed moral fashions on the Vietnam War: it did not create them. Only television executives believe that television made it impossible for the Americans to win the war. If the dominant ethics in television today is that there are no good causes left—only victims of bad causes—there is no guarantee that the medium will not succumb to the next moral fashion. There is even a danger that television's healthy cynicism toward causes will topple into a shallow kind of misanthropy. The ethics of victimhood generate empathy only where victims are obviously blameless. But in modern civil wars—Lebanon in the 1980s, Bosnia and Rwanda in the 1990s—where the distinction between civilian and combatant is often blurred and neighbor kills neighbor, it is difficult to distinguish the innocent and the guilty. Peoples who began as aggressors—the Serbs, for example—often end up as victims. Peoples who had been victims—the Croats and Muslims—become aggressors. The search for blameless victims becomes a fruitless task. The corpses strewn among the rubble seem to make any effort at further comprehension superfluous: here are people locked in a spiral, each with fine reasons for killing each other, each reason as insane as the other. The TV spectacle of corpses encourages a retreat from the attempt to understand.

Where empathy fails to find the blameless victim, the conscience finds comfort in shallow misanthropy. For the reaction—"They're all crazy"—reproduces that reassuring imperial dichotomy between the virtue, moderation, and reasonableness held to exist in the West and the fanaticism and unreason of the East. Here misanthropy shades into amnesia toward all those occasions—Vietnam, the Falklands, the Grenada invasion, Desert Storm—where the same consciences that deride the fanatics of the East found themselves swept up in warlike enthusiasms of their own.

It is not only the victims whose worlds one has to enter, if one wishes to understand modern war, but the world of the gunmen, torturers, and apologists of terror. To such people, the idea that human beings are sacred rights-bearing creatures would be true only for their own. As concerns their enemies and their victims, they have carpentered together persuasive reasons for refusing to think of them as human beings at all. The horror of the world lies not just with the corpses, not just with the consequences, but with the intentions, with the minds of killers. Faced with the deep persuasiveness of ideologies of killing, the temptation to take refuge in moral disgust is strong indeed. Yet disgust is a poor substitute for thought. Television has unfortunate strengths as a medium of moral disgust. As a moral mediator between violent men and the audiences whose attention they crave, television images are more effective at presenting consequences than in exploring intentions; more adept at pointing to the corpses than in explaining why violence may, in certain places, pay so well. As a result, television news bears some responsibility for that generalized misanthropy, that irritable resignation toward the criminal folly of fanatics and assassins, which legitimizes one of the dangerous cultural moods of our time—the feeling that the world has become too crazy to deserve serious reflection.

IV

THUS FAR I have made the following arguments: the moral empathy mediated by television has a history—the emergence of moral universalism in the Western conscience; this universalism has always been in conflict with the intuition that kith and kin have a moral priority over strangers; the twentieth-century inflection of moral universalism has taken the form of an antiideological and antipolitical ethic of siding with the victim; the moral risk entailed by this ethic is misanthropy, a risk and a temptation heightened by television's visual insistence on consequences rather than intentions.

It is time to focus more closely on television news itself, on the impact of its regimes of selection and presentation of the moral relation of viewers to the events it depicts. When we say that watching television is a passive experience, we mean, among other things, that we are unaware of the nature of the visual authority to which we are submitting. Television news is an extremely recent genre: the half-hour news we take for granted is barely thirty years old, and already its codes tend to register subliminally. With increasing familiarity, however, these codes tend to become more evident, more a matter of cultural discussion and interrogation. News is a genre as much as fiction or drama: it is a regime of visual authority, a coercive organization of images according to a stopwatch. Many conventions of television news are taken over from newspapers and radio: that home news is more important than foreign news; that news is about what happened to "the nation" and "the world" in one day; that yesterday's news—yesterday's famine—is no longer news; that some news has to be good news, i.e., that broadcasts should discharge a certain function of good cheer in a cheerless world. To these existing conventions, television has applied two of its own: that news to be news at all must be visual and it must fit into fifteen-, thirty-, and sixty-minute formats. Some of the consequences of these conventions are notorious: The entire script content of the CBS nightly half-hour news would fit on three-quarters of the front page of the *New York Times*. The promiscuity of the nightly news—the jostling together of tornadoes in Pennsylvania, gunmen in Bosnia, striking teachers in Manchester, a royal outing in Suffolk, and infant heart surgery in a California hospital—is dictated by the time constraints of the medium. Yet this jumble of events is presented to the viewer as if it were a representation of the promiscuity of the external world. This incoherence is compounded by the growing importance, across all media, of human-interest stories. The growth of this dimension of the news might once have been understood as a populist counterballast to the dominance of official, governmental information. Yet this populist redefinition of news value to include the curious, the bizarre, and the entertaining has destroyed the coherence of the genre itself so that thoughtful viewers ask themselves at least once a night, "Why am I being shown this? Why is this news?"

The myth sustaining the news is that it is a picture of what happened to "the nation" and "the world" in a given time period, usually the time since the last bulletin. Millions of people look to the screen for signs of their collective identity as a national society and as citizens of one world. The media now play the decisive role in constituting the "imagined community" of nation and globe, the myth that millions of separate "I's" find common identity in a "we." The fiction is that all the events depicted have somehow happened to "us." News editors act as ventriloquists of this "we," serving up a diet of information that is legitimized as being what "we" need to know; in fact, what we get to know is what fits the visual and chronological constraints of the genre. In this circular process, the news is validated as a system of authority, as a national institution with a privileged role as purveyor of the nation's identity and taker of its pulse.

Yet news is not only a system of authority, but also the site of social competition among interest groups and individuals struggling to influence the representation of themselves to the eyes of the watching "we." The struggle over representation has become as important as the struggle for power; indeed, has become the privileged means by which interests fight for power itself. What was once called, in the nineteenth century, the battle for public opinion, conducted within the relatively restricted press read by the middle and upper classes, has become a struggle for "coverage" on a nightly news with a massive and socially heterogeneous audience. Since public opinion polls now exist to tote up individual reaction to this struggle, and since these opinion polls are watched attentively by those in power, the struggle for favorable media coverage has become the key battleground in elections, strikes, and charitable campaigns. In the process, the rationale for news decisions has been put under an intense degree of public scrutiny. Charges of bias are hurled from all sides of the political arena at media executives, while they in turn, faced with this pressure, lean heavily on their journalists to be fair and impartial, which too often means superficial and disengaged.

This focus on political *bias* as the source of the media's distortion of the "we" leaves unaddressed the distorting effect of the news genre itself. News is a mythic narrative of social identity constituted from commodities bought and sold on the international market. The nightly news could be understood as a market in which startling and terrible images compete with each other for ninety-second slots in the bulletin. There is a market in images of horror as there is a market in grain or pork bellies, and there are those who specialize in the production and distribution of such images. Moral intuition might lead one to suppose that such a trade in images of suffering is immoral. There are many goods that are not supposed to be traded, even in a capitalist culture—goods like justice and public office—though they often are. Many societies have attempted to ban the traffic in images of degrading sexuality, but few have attempted to restrict the commerce in images of human suffering. To ban a trade in images of suffering would be to exclude not only disturbing and casual atrocity footage, but also many of the masterpieces of Western art, including Goya's *Horrors of War* and Picasso's *Guernica*. As long as culture itself is a process of market exchange between producers and consumers of images, and as long as we think it wrong for anyone to have the right to dictate the content of these images, then our culture will constantly have to confront the moral ambiguity of making commodities out of other people's pain. Some of the deep ambiguity at the heart of our discomfort in watching scenes of horror on television comes from our knowledge that we are consuming images of other people's suffering, that our moral relations to them are mediated as consumption relations. The shame of voyeurism, therefore, in relation to their suffering has certain unchangeable elements that inhere in the nature of the consumption of representation itself.

Yet certain other components of our shame are susceptible to intervention. The pell-mell competition to fill the nightly news results in a blur of tragedies and crimes—one minute Afghanistan, the next minute Bosnia, then Rwanda, or a bloody train wreck in Kansas—the cumulative effect of which is to create a single banalized commodity of horror. The time disciplines of the news genre militate against the minimum moral requirement of engagement with another person's suffering: that one spends time with them, enough time to pierce the carapace of self-absorption and estrangement that separates us from the moral worlds of others. Moral life is a struggle to see—a struggle against the desire to deny the testimony of one's own eyes and ears. The struggle to believe one's senses is at the heart of the process of moving from voyeurism to commitment. Even eyewitnesses to barbarity, faced with the testimony of their senses, have found themselves fleeing mentally into a fantasy that what they were seeing was some nightmare from which they would awake.

Goya's *Horrors of War* and Picasso's *Guernica* confront this desire to evade the testimony of our own eyes by grounding horror in aesthetic forms that force the spectator to see it as if for the first time. There is no reason to suppose that the news media lack the same capacity of representation to make the real truly real and to force the eye to see, and the conscience to recognize what it has seen. Yet the nightly rhythm of the news militates against this kind of seeing. In the mingling of heterogeneous stories, and in the enforcement of the regime of time, the news makes it impossible to attend to what one has seen. In the end one sees only the news, its personalities, its rules of selection and suppression, its authoritative voice. In the end, the subject of the news is the news itself: what it depicts is a means to the reproduction of its own authoritativeness. In this worship of itself, of its speed, its immense news-gathering resources, its capacity to beat the clock, the news turns all reality into ninety-second exercises in its own style of representation.

A dishonor is done when the flow of television news reduces all the world's horror to identical commodities. In a culture overwhelmed by the volume of promiscuous representation, there must be some practice by which the real—the instant when a real body is struck, abused, or violated—is given a place of special attention, a demarcation that insists that it be *seen.* Anthropologists would call such practices rituals. While it is often said that modern culture is impoverished in sacred ritual, this is not exactly the case. It certainly has its own fetishisms—money and consumption—and, for all the surface din of moral controversy, a generally shared belief in the special respect due the human person. The idea that the person is sacred, in property, rights, and life, is widely shared, if honored more in the breach than in the observance. Whether the world we live in is any more violent, any more full of suffering, is, in the nature of things, impossible to decide. What seems less disputable is that the culture is less able to satisfy human needs for an account of our dignity as creatures, less able to treat the human experience of violence and suffering with the respect it deserves.

The skeptic might well reply that if the television audience wants moral reassurance, it should turn to the churches: television's business is news, not piety; information, not sermons. The sacred is not its domain. This reply would be adequate if it were true, if television worshiped at no altars other than the search for information. The claim that television should pay some respect to suffering would be irrelevant if the medium paid no respect to anything at all. Yet while television news publicly adheres to the skeptic's code of honor—that nothing is sacred—in practice it worships power. Television is the church of modern authority. Consider, for example, the television broadcasts of the 1953 British coronation, the funeral of John F. Kennedy, the funeral of Winston Churchill, the marriage of Prince Charles and Lady Diana Spencer, or the inauguration of presidents. These are the sacred occasions of modern secular culture, and television has devised its own rhetoric and ritual to enfold viewers in a sense of the sacred importance of these moments: the hushed voices of the commentators; loving attention to uniform and vestments of power; above all, the tacit inference that what is being represented is a rite of national significance.

If, then, television is capable of treating power as sacred, it becomes plausible for us to ask it to treat suffering with equal respect. If television can jettison its schedules and transform its discourse for the sake of a wedding or a funeral, then we can ask it to do the same for famine or genocide. If television does know how to liberate itself from the news regime, then it becomes possible to ask it to reconsider the adequacy of the news regime as a whole. It becomes slightly less utopian at least to pose the question whether television should have news at all. Serving up the world in ninety-second slices is, on television journalists' own admission, a poor second-best to the explanatory power of a good newspaper. In moments of self-doubt and self-examination, good television journalists will admit that if the general population were entirely dependent on their nightly bulletin for their understanding of the world, they would be exceedingly poorly informed. Perhaps the logic of these doubts should be pushed further. Television does some things supremely well. The best documentaries sometimes achieve the prerequisite of moral vision itself; they force the spectator to see, to shed the carapace of cliché and to encounter alien worlds in all their mystery and complexity. There is almost never an occasion when the time formats of news bulletins allow even the best journalist to do the same. When the rules of a genre are in such contradiction to the needs and intentions of those trying to make best use of it, there is a case for scrapping the genre altogether. If the nightly news were replaced by magazine programs and documentary features, the institutional preconditions for a journalism that respects itself and the terrible events it covers would begin to exist. Such a journalism would be forced to take the hardest part of a journalist's job—selection—very seriously. It would have to discard as many stories as it chose to cover, and it would have to change its conception of what a story is. It would have to challenge accepted definitions of newsworthiness to intervene before starvation becomes famine, before torture becomes genocide, before racist persecution becomes mass expulsion, and religious conflict becomes civil war. It would have to get to the scene, in other words, before the ambulances arrive. Such a journalism might then be able to challenge other coercive features of its own genre: for example, the newsroom rule of thumb that one British,

American, or European life is worth—in news value—a hundred Asian or African lives. As the charitable response to images of horror makes plain, the medium itself is helping to generate an international awareness that has less and less patience with these kinds of discriminations.

Utopian, no doubt. Yet let us at least be clear that the grounds for wishing this utopia into existence are moral. Whether it wishes or not, television has become the principal mediation between the suffering of strangers and the consciences of those in the world's few remaining zones of safety. No matter how assiduously its managers assert that the medium's function is merely informative, they cannot escape the moral consequences of their power. It has become not merely the means through which we see each other, but the means by which we shoulder each other's fate. If the regimes of representation by which it mediates these relations dishonor the suffering they depict, then the cost is measured not only in shame, but in human lives.

The Narcissism of Minor Difference

I

MIRKOVCI, MARCH 1993, 4:00 A.M. Mirkovci is a village in eastern Croatia that was cut in two by the Serb-Croat war between September 1991 and January 1992. Full-scale ethnic war has shifted south to Bosnia, but here, every night, Serb and Croat militias, dug in around Mirkovci, still exchange small-arms fire and the occasional bazooka round. I am in an abandoned farmhouse basement that serves as the command post of the local Serbian militia. The Croatians are about two hundred and fifty yards away, somewhere in the darkness.

This is a village war. The men on either side of the front line once were neighbors. The Serbs on guard duty—most of them tired, middle-aged reservists, who'd much rather be in bed—all went to school with the Croats, just as tired, probably just as middle-aged, in the bunker close by. Before the war, they had been to the same schools, worked in the same garage, went with the same girls. In the last national census of Yugoslavia, taken in 1990, the town of Vukovar, which is about twenty miles away, and the villages nearby had rates of ethnic intermarriage as high as 30 percent. Nearly a quarter of the population claimed their nationality as Yugoslav, that is, as belonging to neither Croat, Serb, nor Muslim.

There are about a dozen soldiers in the farmhouse. From time to time, one of them slings his rifle on his shoulder and tramps up and down in a slit trench that cuts through the gardens and clotheslines. The rest sit on army cots, gossiping, smoking, dozing, and cleaning their weapons. Most of them are reservists, but there is a paramilitary called Chobi who wears a black toque emblazoned with the motto SERBIA: LIBERTY OR DEATH. He calls up an old friend on the CB radio. "Ustashe," he taunts, "are you still going with that girl?" "Why should I tell you?" the Croat replies: "Chetnik psychopath." Pleasantries continue, and then they hang up. They talk on the phone most evenings, it appears.

I've been sitting with them most of the night while they doze, play cards, clean their weapons. I want to understand how neighbors are turned into enemies, how people who once had a lot in common end up having nothing in common but war. Wherever I've seen this process happen—in Afghanistan, Rwanda, Northern Ireland—I've found it puzzling. I've never accepted the idea that nationalist war is an eruption of tribal hatreds and ancient enmities. Theorists like Samuel Huntington would lead me to believe that there is a fault line running through the back gardens of Mirkovci, with the Croats in the bunker representing the civilization of the Catholic Roman West and the Serbs nearby representing Byzantium, Orthodoxy, and the Cyrillic East. Certainly that is how the more self-inflated ideologues on either side see the conflict. But at worm's-eye level, here in Mirkovci, I don't see civilizational fault lines, geological templates that have split apart. These metaphors take for granted what needs to be explained: how neighbors once ignorant of the very idea that they belong to opposed civilizations begin to think—and hate—in these terms; how they vilify and demonize people they once called friends; how, in short, the seeds of mutual paranoia are sown, grain by grain, on the soil of a common life.

On the bunk next to me, leaning against the wall, wearing combat fatigues, is a compact and dapper middle-aged man with bright, wily eyes and a thick, stylish mustache. With a certain false naiveté, I venture the thought that I can't tell Serbs and Croats apart. "What makes you think you're so different?"

He looks scornful and takes a cigarette pack out of his khaki jacket. "See this? These are Serbian cigarettes. Over there," he says, gesturing out the window, "they smoke Croatian cigarettes."

"But they're both cigarettes, right?"

"Foreigners don't understand anything." He shrugs and resumes cleaning his Zastovo machine pistol.

But the question I've asked bothers him, so a couple of minutes later he tosses the weapon on the bunk between us and says, "Look, here's how it is. Those Croats, they think they're better than us. They want to be the gentlemen. Think they're fancy Europeans. I'll tell you something. We're all just Balkan shit."

First he tells me that Croats and Serbs have nothing in common. Everything about them is different, down to their cigarettes. A minute later, he tells me that the real problem with Croats is that they think they're "better than us." Finally, he decides: We're actually all the same.

Yes, civilizational antagonisms are present in what he says, but they are part of an ambiguous dialogue between myth and experience, fantasy and reality. It is as if the nationalist myth—Serbs and Croats are radically distinct peoples with nothing in common—is struggling with this man's lived experience that, really, not much distinguishes him from his Croat neighbors. The two planes of consciousness—the political and the personal—coexist but do not confront each other. Somewhere in him, there is a sliver of doubt that might lead to questioning and even refusal, but there are no newspapers, no radio stations, no alternative language in which he can frame his doubts and discover that others have doubts just like him. So the contradictions float around in his head. In the watches of the night, he waits, tense and restless, for the next mortar round. Firing off a few rounds may be a way of resolving the tension. To hell with it, he may curse. They don't pay me to think. Let's keep it simple. Violence does that, at least: it keeps things simple.

There is nothing timeless about this man's national identity. It's not some primordial essence, formed by history and tradition, latent within, waiting to carry him off to war. For him, identity is primarily a relational term. A Serb is someone who is not a Croat. A Croat is someone who is not a Serb. But when difference is relational, it is also an empty tautology. We are not what we are not. My dapper Serbian soldier simply cannot tell me what he is fighting for, other than his own survival. But survival doesn't entirely explain why he is here, because he knows perfectly well that until a few years ago, his survival was not in question. How it has become so, why he now lives in a community of fear, united in hatred against another community of fear, is ultimately as mysterious to him as it is to me.

Nationalist ideology tries to fill this void inside him; tries to give the foot soldiers a reason to fight and die. But whatever this particular Serb has heard on his radio or read in his local paper does not swallow up the identity formed by his own personal experience. The fit between national and personal identity is imperfect. The black-toqued ethnic paramilitaries may be true believers, but ordinary people—the foot soldiers of ethnic war like him—dimly, sometimes agonizingly, perceive the gap between what they see with their own eyes and what they are told to believe.

Nationalism does not simply "express" a preexistent identity: it "constitutes" a new one. It would be false to the history of this part of the world to maintain that ethnic antagonisms were simply waiting, like the magma beneath a volcano, for a template to shift, a fissure to split open. It is an abuse of anthropological terminology to call Serbs and Croats ethnic groups at all: they speak more or less the same language; they are from the same racial stock of the south Balkan Slavs. There are differences between them, particularly in their family names, but these differences are nearly invisible to outsiders. In crude terms, you cannot tell them apart. Even if we allow ourselves to call them ethnic groups, the kind of Serb this man believes himself to have been before the descent into war is not the kind of Serb he became after the war. Before the war, he might have thought of himself as a Yugoslav or a café manager or a husband rather than as a Serb. Now as he sits in this farmhouse bunker, there are men two hundred and fifty yards away who would kill him. For them he is only a Serb, not a neighbor, not a friend, not a Yugoslav, not a former teammate at the football club. And because he is only a Serb for his enemies, he has become only a Serb to himself.

Nationalism is a fiction: it requires the willing suspension of disbelief. To believe in nationalist fictions is to forget certain realities. In this Serbian soldier's case, it means forgetting that he was once a neighbor, brother, and friend to the people in the next trench. But how does nationalism "constitute"/create identity?

How did nationalism rework this particular man's identity? We need to find a story that will explain how communities of fear are created out of communities of interest, a story that will connect the collapse of state power and the rise of nationalist paranoia down at the human level, in places like Mirkovci.

II

FROM 1945 TO 1991 neighbors lived together in a state called Yugoslavia. There were differences between Serbs and Croats—one was Orthodox, the other Catholic—and a history of bad blood, a vivid memory of Croatian Ustashe persecution of ethnic minority Serbs in Croatia during World War II. There was a state, presided over by Tito, that held power by combining intimidation with appeals to "brotherhood and unity" among ethnic groups. The history of interethnic war between 1941 and 1945 was systematically repressed, and Tito did his best to prevent any one ethnic group from dominating the institutions of the federal state, though by the end, the Serbs occupied most of the leadership posts in the Yugoslav National Army. This strategy of "divide and rule," coupled with calls for "brotherhood and unity," did have a certain popular legitimacy. Many Yugoslavs of the 1960s and 1970s sincerely thought they had put ethnic hatred behind them. Where ethnic difference was stressed—by Croatian nationalists, for example—it was repressed. By 1990, the generation traumatized by World War II was beginning to die and the poisons of the past were leaching away. In a village like Mirkovci, "brotherhood and unity" actually meant a good deal of ethnic intermarriage, and while Serbs and Croats went to different churches, they did work together in local institutions. The most important of these was the police station. If you had a problem, if someone stole your car radio, the police didn't ask your nationality first. You weren't necessarily offered an efficient process; but at least you weren't subjected to ethnic justice.

Then in May 1980 Tito died. States whose legitimacy depends on the personal charisma of one individual can *only* fall apart when that individual dies. Tito was the last of the Hapsburgs, the last ruler of the south Balkan peninsula with the legitimacy and the guile to make divide-and-rule work. After his death, power began to ebb away from the center to the Communist elites in the republics. But these elites now felt the legitimacy of their own authority eroding. Without Tito, they became little more than networks of corrupt ethnic patronage. By 1989, the collapse of Communism lent an edge of panic to their search for legitimacy. Throughout Eastern Europe, after 1989, Communist parties tried to convert themselves into social democratic electoral machines. Theirs was a pantomime act, but however insincere, it did help to create what the electorates of these societies wanted, a "normal" (i.e., pluralistic) political system. Such was the path taken by former Communists in East Germany, Hungary, Ukraine, and Poland; they accepted the vernacular of democracy and appealed to citizens as individual voters. The question is, Why did this liberal civic vision, which was available in Yugoslavia, never take hold? Why were the Yugoslav elites incapable even of democratic pantomime? For the appeal of the liberal political option ought to have been much stronger. Tito allowed Yugoslavs to travel; they came back with some idea of how democracy looked and sounded. Yugoslavia enjoyed one of the freest civil societies in Eastern Europe, with opposition journals, philosophical discussion groups like the Belgrade Circle, a vivid café life, art, theater, and cinema. In retrospect, it seems clear that the relative freedom of this civil society was in fact the source of its weakness. The opposition existed on sufferance; it knew, in its heart of hearts, that it was one of Tito's cunning indulgences. It was a cultural opposition, not a political opposition. It never challenged the regime in the name of an explicitly democratic vision. The illusion that, under Tito, things were better than they were elsewhere in Eastern Europe co-opted the opposition and prevented it from mobilizing people as citizens. In nearby Czechoslovakia much harsher police repression taught the opposition to expect nothing from the regime; taught it that cultural freedoms of the type enjoyed by the Yugoslavs meant little unless they also enjoyed political power. The Yugoslav opposition never benefited, to use Timothy Garton Ash's phrase, from the "uses of adversity." Tito's relative indulgence emasculated the opposition. They failed to find a plausible rhetoric of interethnic appeal to replace "brotherhood and unity." By 1990, more than a quarter of the Yugoslav population identified themselves as "Yugoslavs." This was the constituency that might have been mobilized by the opposition in all the republics in defense of multiethnic politics. But by then, the Communist system had so balkanized politics, republic by republic, that the civic oppositions in each of them could never get together to marshal a common defense of civic values against the ethnic nationalism that was pulling the country apart. By then, Communism was collapsing, and the heroes of the hour were those who had suffered under Communism, which in Yugoslavia's case were the nationalists like Tudjman in Croatia.

In the mid-1980s, the Communist elite left in place after Tito's death realized that the dictator's departure and the inner decay of Communism required them to invent a new language of popular appeal. Even in a one-party state, a new rhetoric was needed to mobilize the public. The fact that Serbs had been slowly reduced to ethnic minority status in the hilly southwestern region of Kosovo provided Serbian leader Milosevic with just such a rallying cry. Ethnic Albanians made up 90 percent of the population, and they were demanding independence or annexation to nearby Albania. Serbs might have accepted minority status were it not that Kosovo occupied such a central place in the Serbian imagination: it was where their most ancient and beautiful medieval churches were located, and Kosovo field was the site of the fateful battle with the Turks in 1389 that led to five centuries of Turkish imperial occupation. Until the 1980s, most Serbs ignored the condition of their cousins in backward Kosovo. But the five-hundredth anniversary of the defeat at Kosovo provided Milosevic with an opportunity to claim that Kosovo remained the heartland of Serbian national life, despite the fact that few Serbs actually lived there anymore.

It is doubtful that Milosevic actually took the cause of Kosovo to his heart. For him, nationalist demagoguery was a language game, a rhetorical strategy for electoral survival in the uncertain world of the post-Titoist succession battle. He was apparently surprised that he had chanced upon a winning formula. During a meeting with Kosovan Serbs, who were protesting ethnic Albanian demands for independence or autonomy, Milosevic remarked, apparently off the cuff, that "they will never beat you again." Since it was ethnic Albanians rather than Serbs who were being beaten by Milosevic's police, the remark was a curious inversion of realities, but it did tap into deep reservoirs of Serb self-pity: a victim nation, who had fought for liberty against the Turks, who had fought the Austrians, who had been persecuted by the Ustashe, who had been prevented by Tito—a Croat—from dominating the federal Yugoslavia, and who were now suffering at the hands of a Muslim majority in their own heartland. This combustible mixture of genuine grievance and self-pitying paranoia was ignited by Milosevic's remark, and by his subsequent program to annul the autonomy of Kosovo and reabsorb it within the Serbian republic. Moreover, in the mid-1980s, Serbian self-pity and frustrated dreams of historical grandeur coincided with a deepening economic crisis. The nationalist dream of reuniting Serbs within one state not only provided a Communist elite with a language of electoral mobilization, but offered a diversion. It was a politics of fantasy, leading the population away from real issues, such as the deepening economic difficulties of Serbia and the stubborn backwardness of the south Balkans. The Greater Serbian project was a fantasy at another level too. Because of the dispersion of the Serbian population within adjacent republics, the project of reunifying the Serbs (or any other ethnic group for that matter) could be achieved only by forcible population transfer, by ethnic cleansing.

This implication of Serbian aggrandizement was evident to the elites of neighboring republics. The Yugoslav republics each began demanding states of their own, and as they did so, the ethnic minorities in each began to wonder: Who will protect us now? This was the question my Serb soldier now asked himself. As Croatia moved toward full independence in 1990, he saw the Serbs being dismissed from the local police station by the new Croatian government. The prospect of ethnic justice came into view, and however much the Croatian nationalists denied it, they did intend to demote the Serbs in Croatia from the status of a founding nationality of a federal republic into an ethnic minority subject to ethnic majority rule. Didn't the new Croatia call itself, in its new constitution, the state of the Croatian people? Where did that leave the people who lived in Croatia but were not Croats?

This dawning realization is the turning point in the whole story. Interethnic accommodation anywhere depends on an equilibrium of forces. An ethnic minority can live in peace with an ethnic majority as long as that majority does not use its preponderance to turn the institutions of the state into an instrument of ethnic favoritism or ethnic justice. In the Yugoslav case, the liberal alternative—in which no ethnic group, as such, has collective power or privileges, and in which all individuals have equal rights—was not available. National independence for the Croats meant ethnic minority subservience for the Serbs in Croatia. It was the fear of domination that imbued the consciousness of the Serbs with paranoia. The Serbian soldier would have read in his Serb newspaper about the atrocities the Croats committed against the Serbs during the second World War, only forty-five miles away at the concentration camp called Jasenovac. He'd heard something about this before, but now he paid attention. Now atrocity stories began to generate a self-pitying collective myth, which seeped into his own self-description. For the first time, the dapper Serbian reservist began to think: I can't trust my neighbors, and come to think of it, we've always been different. He hadn't been to an Orthodox service since his own christening, but now he remembered that, after all, "we" are Orthodox; "they" are Catholic. As the Serbian radio from Belgrade and Milosevic's television stations dinned into him the proposition that Serbs could be safe only inside their own nation, he began to think that they were right. By late 1990, the Titoist state was visibly disintegrating around him: at the local police station, all the Serbs had been dismissed. On the town councils in his region, Croatian teams, loyal to Franjo Tudjman's party, had taken over, and there were rumors among the Krajina Serbs, as the Serb minority in Croatia was called, that the Croatians were stockpiling arms and secretly training at night against the day they declared full independence and Belgrade retaliated by sending in the tanks. At this point, local Serbian warlords—ex-police and army mostly—

began to appear, and they told him: Tito is dead; the Croats are taking power; you've nobody but us to protect you. Soon, he was working for the warlords, spending his nights in an abandoned farmhouse trading shots with people he once called friends. In the space of three years, he had been delivered back four hundred years to the late feudal world before the European nation-state began. In three years, he had been delivered from civilization—from interethnic tolerance and accommodation—to the Hobbesian world of interethnic war.

Note here the causative order: first the collapse of the overarching state, then Hobbesian fear, and only then nationalist paranoia, followed by warfare. Disintegration of the state comes first, nationalist paranoia comes next. Nationalist sentiment on the ground, among common people, is a secondary consequence of political disintegration, a response to the collapse of state order and the interethnic accommodation that it made possible. Nationalism creates communities of fear, groups held together by the conviction that their security depends on sticking together. People become "nationalistic" when they are afraid; when the only answer to the question "Who will protect me now?" becomes "my own people."

What I've tried to do here is tell a story that connects the top and the bottom—the elite and the people—in a common narrative. But a major puzzle remains. If Hobbesian fear explains why neighbors turn into enemies, what explains that earlier shift in which identities that were once permeable begin to be sealed off? How did people begin to think of themselves as Serbs and Croats to the exclusion of all else? For nearly fifty years, being a Serb or being a Croat took second place to being a Yugoslav; sometimes it took third or fourth place to being a worker or a mother, or any of the other identities that constitute the range of our belonging.

Nationalism denies that multiple belonging is possible. It insists on the primacy of national belonging over all other allegiances. But how does it do this? Here we need to take a theoretical detour and think more carefully about difference itself, to ask how difference, which is always comparative and relational, can change with such suddenness.

III

THE TRANSFORMATION of brothers into enemies has puzzled the human imagination at least since Genesis. For Genesis begins the story of mankind not with a murder between strangers, but between brothers. It is precisely because the difference between them is so slight that the roots of the crime remain so mysterious. One brother is a keeper of sheep; the other a tiller of the ground. Both make sacrifices to the Lord: one finds favor; the other does not. We are not told why God's blessing should be so partial. God merely informs the disappointed brother that he must be content with his lot and not contest the inscrutable partiality of Providence.

Again, for reasons unknown, the older brother refuses to submit to God's judgment. Consumed by rage at God's injustice and envy toward his younger brother's unaccountable good fortune, he lures that brother into a field. There, with his bare hands, or with weapons unspecified, he takes his brother's life. God, needless to say, is watching. When challenged, Cain denies the crime—and also denies his human kinship:

"Am I my brother's keeper?"

Significantly, Cain is not destroyed for his crime, but marked as an outcast and banished east of Eden. There he becomes a founder of nations, and since his authority began with a murder, crime and countercrime unfold in the dire downward logic of revenge. "If Cain shall be avenged sevenfold, truly Lamech seventy and seven fold." It is this logic that so disgusts God that he decides to flood the world and save only Noah and his flock.

In her fine study, the biblical scholar Regina Schwartz identifies what is so truly mysterious about the story: the scarcity of God's mercy. Why can't he bless both Cain and Abel? Why must one be chosen and the other excluded? Why, when both are the same, must one be cast out? This, she argues, is the logic of monotheistic systems of belief. Scarcity, she writes, is "encoded in the Bible as a principle of Oneness (one land, one people, one nation) and in monotheistic thinking (one Deity), it becomes a demand of exclusive allegiance that threatens with the violence of exclusion." One nation under God: the exclusionary drives of nationalism seem to derive—though how exactly we do not know—from this idea that only one people can be chosen, only one brother can find favor, while all the others must languish under the mark of Cain. What's more, election and violence go hand in hand because the self-righteousness of election is always shadowed by the terror that one might just as well have been visited with the mark of Cain. Better to visit the mark of Cain on others, lest it be stamped on your own brow.

But the story of Cain and Abel is not just about the baffling scarcity of God's mercy and the human conviction—or terror— that God's mercy, if mysteriously granted, can also just as mysteriously be withheld. It is also, at the simplest level, about brothers—about the paradox that brothers can hate each other more passionately than strangers can; that the emotions stirred up within commonality are more violent than those aroused by pure and radical difference. In a few short verses of Genesis, two persons of the same blood end up not recognizing each other as the same flesh. The story of Cain seems to say, at its simplest, that there are no wars more savage than civil wars, no hatreds more intractable than those between the closest kin.

IV

TOWARD THE END of the First World War, in a mood of melancholy misanthropy, Sigmund Freud began to turn his attention to the phenomenon of group aggression, and in particular, to a paradox that he had observed in his clinical practice. In 1917, in the course of an essay titled "The Taboo of Virginity," he observed in passing that "it is precisely the minor differences in people who are otherwise alike that form the basis of feelings of strangeness and hostility between them." He went on that "it would be tempting to pursue this idea and to derive from this 'narcissism of minor differences' the hostility which in every human relation we see fighting against feelings of fellowship and overpowering the commandment that all men should love one another."

The common elements humans share seem less essential to their perceptions of their own identities than the marginal "minor" elements that divide them. What Marx called "species being"—our identity as members of the human race—counts for relatively little. Men share a common genetic inheritance with women, down to a chromosome or two, and yet it is difference rather than commonality that has always been salient, so much so that undeniably common features—such as mental capacity—have been construed as unequal, notwithstanding all evidence to the contrary. What was puzzling to Freud is why this differentiation process should be accompanied by such large amounts of anxiety. Why is it that men's identities depend on the constitution of woman as an object, not merely of desire, but of fear? "Perhaps this dread is based on the fact that woman is different from man," Freud wrote, "forever incomprehensible and mysterious, strange and therefore apparently hostile. The man is afraid of being weakened by the woman, infected with her femininity and of then showing himself incapable." Strange and therefore hostile— why is it that minor difference should be strange *and therefore* threatening?

When Freud returned to the "narcissism of minor differences" five years later, in "Group Psychology and the Analysis of the Ego," his analysis had shifted from sexual to group differences. Even in intimate groups, he wrote, "friendship, marriage, the relations between parents and children"—emotions of hostility and suspicion competed with feelings of human kinship. Here too "species identity" and even long-standing emotional bonds are never sufficient to entirely overcome feelings of hostility. The same phenomenon was observable between societies and nations. The closer the relation between human groups, the more hostile they were likely to be toward each other:

> Of two neighboring towns each is the other's most jealous rival; every little canton looks down upon the others with contempt. Closely related races keep one another at arm's length; the South German cannot endure the North German, the Englishman casts every kind of aspersion upon the Scot, the Spaniard despises the Portuguese. We are no longer astonished that greater differences should lead to an almost insuperable repugnance, such as the Gallic people feel for the German, the Aryan for the Semite and the white races for the colored.

As he broadened his analysis to include national and racial difference, Freud seemed to muddy the distinction between major and minor difference. It seems an error to suppose that some human differences, say race or gender, are intrinsically more important than others, like class or national identity. Gender and racial difference are certainly minor relative to the overwhelming genetic commonality that unites men and women and persons of different races, but they become major when used as markers of power and status. No human difference matters much until it becomes a privilege, until it becomes the basis for oppression. Power is the vector that turns minor into major.

Moreover, what looks like a minor difference when seen from the outside may feel like a major difference when seen from the inside. What Freud's distinction, for all its imprecision, helps us to see is that the level of hostility and intolerance between groups bears no relation to the size of their cultural, historical, or physical differences as measured by a dispassionate outside observer. Indeed, the smaller these differences may seem to outsiders, the larger they may loom in insiders' mutual self-definitions.

For Freud such antagonistic self-definition was connected to "narcissism":

> In the undisguised antipathies and aversion which people
> feel towards strangers with whom they have to do we may
> recognize the expression of self-love—of narcissism. This
> self-love works for the preservation of the individual, and
> behaves as though the occurrence of any divergence from
> his own particular lines of development involved a criti-
> cism of them and a demand for their alteration.

Freud's analysis focuses our attention on the paradoxical relation between narcissism and aggression. It is precisely because the differences between groups are minor that they must be expressed aggressively. The less substantial the differences between two groups, the more they both struggle to portray those differences as absolute. Moreover, the aggression that is required to hold a group together is not only directed outward at another group, but directed inward at eliminating the differences that distinguish individual from group. Individuals, Freud is saying, pay a psychic price for group belonging. They must turn the aggressive desire to conform against their own individuality. In order to dissolve his identity in Serbdom, for example, the foot soldier must repress his own individuality *and* his memory of common ties with former Croatian friends. He must do a certain violence to himself to make the mask of hatred fit.

By extrapolating a little from Freud, it becomes possible to think of nationalism as a kind of narcissism. A nationalist takes the neutral facts about a people—their language, habitat, culture, tradition, and history—and turns these facts into a narrative, whose purpose is to illuminate the self-consciousness of a group, to enable them to think of themselves as a nation with a claim to self-determination. A nationalist, in other words, takes "minor differences"—indifferent in themselves—and transforms them into major differences. For this purpose, traditions are invented, a glorious past is gilded and refurbished for public consumption, and a people who might not have thought of themselves as a people at all suddenly begin to dream of themselves as a nation. Viewing nationalism as a kind of narcissism reveals the projective and self-regarding quality of the nationalistic discourse. Nationalism is a distorting mirror in which believers see their simple ethnic, religious, or territorial attributes transformed into glorious attributes and qualities. Though Freud does not explain exactly how this happens, the systematic overvaluation of the self results in systematic devaluation of strangers and outsiders. In this way narcissistic self-regard depends upon and in turn exacerbates intolerance.

Again, the facts of difference themselves are neutral: there is nothing genetically coded about the antagonisms between ethnicities, races, and genders. Differences of language, tradition, and history may be a matter of relative insignificance if there is some form of political settlement between ethnic groups, some overarching state that guarantees that all can go about their business without fearing for their security. In conditions of peace, considerable blurring of ethnic boundaries may occur. People center their identities on their individuality, rather than on their ethnicity. They become husbands or wives, lovers or friends first, and members of a group second.

But since identity is relational, any activation of group pride in one group is bound to activate it in another. Initially, the narcissist competition between groups may take comparatively innocent forms, so long as there is a state to guarantee security for both. Processions, marches, speeches that have no provocative intent but the awakening of group pride may set in train emulative display by the other side. Once these displays of group pride begin to include claims to territory, demands for self-determination, revisiting of old grievances and hurts, the cycle of narcissism begins to pass beyond emulation into antagonism.

The particular property of the narcissist gaze is that it glances up at the Other only to confirm its difference. Then it looks down again and turns its gaze upon itself. It does not *engage* with the Other in any real sense. Narcissist anxiety expresses itself chiefly in passive self-absorption. A narcissist is uninterested in others except to the extent that they reflect back upon himself. What is different is rejected if it fails to confirm the narcissist in his self-opinion.

In the original Greek myth, Narcissus is the archetype of passive absorption. He wastes away, staring at his own reflection in the water, oblivious to the world. Freud does not explain why the same self-absorbed figure can suddenly come awake from his daze and attack those who break into his reverie. But in connecting self-absorption to a capacity for aggression, Freud does help us to detect a connection between narcissism and nationalist intolerance. Intolerant people are actively uninterested in learning about those they purport to despise. Freud helps us to see this form of closed-mindedness as a narcissistic defense and intolerance as a self-referential system in which a narcissist uses the external world only to confirm his essential beliefs. It is the narcissistic investment in intolerance that makes it so uniquely unresponsive to rational argument. In that Serbian bunker, I heard reservists say that they disliked breathing the same air as Croatians, disliked being in the same room with them. There was some threatening uncleanness about them. And this from men who only two years before had not even thought that the air they breathed belonged to one group or the other.

V

BUT WE ARE GETTING ahead of ourselves, for this kind of narcissistic imperviousness occurs only late in the process when two groups are already redescribing each other as enemies. In the first stages, there is rather ambivalence, conflict within identity itself, feelings of difference fighting against feelings of recognition—the very process under way when the Serbian soldier told me that really, the Serbs and the Croats were all the same. It is not a sense of radical difference that leads to conflict with others, but the refusal to admit a moment of recognition. Violence must be done to the self before it can be done to others. Living tissue of connection and recognition must be cauterized before a neighbor is reinvented as an enemy.

No such violence to the self is necessary if one assumes that national identities are givens, archaic entities that require only an infusion of fear to stir them into life. In *The Clash of Civilizations,* Samuel Huntington is not surprised by the violence that overtook Yugoslavia. It is liberal "secular myopia," he argues, to think that ethnic difference is minor. Ethnicity is built upon religious or confessional differences, Catholic versus Orthodox. "Millennia of human history have shown that religion is not a 'small difference,' " he asserts, "but possibly the most profound difference that can exist between people. The frequency, intensity and violence of fault line wars are greatly enhanced by beliefs in different gods."

But it is hardly "secular myopia" to point out that in the Balkans, at least fifty years of official secularism by the Communist regime together with the more effective secularization made possible by economic modernization had substantially eroded the hold of organized religion. Certainly, priests and relics figure in the nationalist revival in both Serbia and Croatia, but again at the worm's-eye level, the salient process is the emptying-out of the symbolic vessels of religious difference. True, some ethnic paramilitaries went to war wearing Orthodox or Catholic crosses as personal jewelry. True, the gunners on each side made a particular point of targeting the churches, minarets, mosques, and burial grounds of the other side. But what is striking is the inauthenticity, shallowness, and fraudulence of their religious convictions. The militiamen I talked to said they were defending their families; they never once said they were defending their faith. Huntington takes the violence in the Balkans as proof that religious differences were "major" and fundamental. The argument could be stood on its head: It was precisely because the religious differences were fading away that they triggered such an exaggerated defense. It was not because religion triggered deep feelings, but because it triggered inauthentic ones, that it helped to unleash such a tumult of violent self-righteousness.

These are the sorts of paradoxes that make the tragedy puzzling, even to those who lived through it. Nearly everyone—with the exception of a minority of nationalist true believers—expresses surprise at the astonishing rapidity with which fifty years of ethnic coexistence was destroyed, perhaps forever. Groups of survivors huddle in the ruins of what was once a common life and ask themselves, How did we bring the root down upon ourselves? At its most basic, the surprise is metaphysical: If we are all human beings, they seem to be saying, how did we do this to each other?

Needless to say, one needn't take their surprise at face value. When expressed to foreigners, surprise is an easy pledge of allegiance to the family of man, and it need not rule out banal bestiality toward the family next door. There is a little verse by G. K. Chesterton that refers to "the villas and chapels where / I learned with little labour / The way to love my fellow man / And hate my next door neighbour." Abstract humanism can happily coexist with loathing for actual human beings. To think well of oneself, at least in this century, it is necessary to believe in moral universals; to protect oneself, on the other hand, it may be necessary to hate and to legitimize this hatred with intense forms of moral particularism. The conflict between the particular and the universal is usually resolved by deciding that, while all human beings deserve equal moral consideration, really, one's neighbors do not deserve to be called human beings at all. Long before a shot was fired in

Yugoslavia, the media of both Croatia and Serbia were readying their populations to think of the other side as vermin, insects, dogs, and other noisome creatures. Again, however, dehumanization requires an especially assiduous creation of narcissist fictions. Croats and Serbs look the same, walk on two legs, share unmistakable human attributes. How does the fantasy of dehumanization overcome the evidence of common humanity? Once the killing has started, dehumanization is easily accomplished: the fact that the other side has killed your own defines them as nonhuman and then legitimizes nonhuman behavior on your part. The puzzle comes earlier: How is dehumanization achieved *before* the shooting starts? It is fear that turns minor difference into major, that makes the gulf between ethnicities into a distinction between species, between human and inhuman. And not just fear, but guilt as well. For if you have shared a common life with another group and then suddenly begin to fear them, because they suddenly have power over you, you have to overcome the weight of happy memory; you have to project onto *them* the blame for destroying a common life.

The narcissism of minor difference may not *explain* why communities of fear begin to loathe each other. It is not an explanatory theory. It is only a phrase, with a certain heuristic usefulness. Its virtue is that it doesn't take ethnic antagonism as a given; it doesn't accept differing histories or origins as a fate that dictates bloody outcomes. It draws our attention to the projective and fantastic quality of ethnic identities, to their particular inauthenticity. It suggests that it is precisely their inauthenticity that triggers violent reactions of defense. It also helps us to notice their dynamic nature. Ethnicity is sometimes described as if it were skin, a fate that cannot be changed. In fact, what is essential about ethnicity is its plasticity. It is not a skin, but a mask, constantly repainted.

The most useful element of Freud's idea is the perception that as external differences between groups diminish, symbolic differences become more salient. As less and less distinguishes you from anybody else, the more important it becomes to wear the differentiating mask. Croats and Serbs drove the same cars; they worked in the same German factories as *gasturbeiters;* they longed to build the same folkloric Swiss chalets on the outskirts of town and raise the same vegetables in the same back gardens. Modernization—to use a big, ugly word—has drawn their styles of life together. They probably have more in common with each other than their peasant grandparents had, especially since their grandparents were believers, and belief might well have been a real source of division. But the grandsons haven't gone to church for years. Modernity—the real life they have been living since 1960 at least—has been steadily reducing the differences between them. Nonetheless, nationalism has turned the imagined differences between them into an abyss, which can be filled only with gunfire. On both sides of the barricades, young men fight to maintain ethnic difference, both dressed in the same international uniform: the tight-fitting combat fatigues, designer shades, and headbands popularized by Sylvester Stallone's Rambo.

If this is so, one cannot assume that rising real incomes, modernization, homogenization, secularization, the gradual leveling-up of regions of backwardness can be counted on to reduce ethnic friction and intolerance. Indeed, although perhaps only as a transitional phenomenon, modernization may exacerbate relations between ethnic groups and lead to an increase in intolerance. Modernization gives them spoils to fight over, and if modernization raises all incomes but does not reduce economic disparities between ethnic groups, it may exacerbate their competition. Even when modernization benefits all groups, it may still send them scurrying back toward the ghetto of fantasized identities. Reduction of "objective" difference between competing groups does not necessarily, and by itself, lead to a reduction in "subjective" suspicion. Indeed, as groups converge "objectively," their mutual intolerance may grow. This helps to explain why nationalist revivals are not confined to poor or peripheral states and why growing prosperity does not buy off nationalist discontent.

Globalism scours away distinctiveness at the surface of our identities and forces us back into ever more assertive defense of the inner differences—language, mentality, myth, and fantasy—that escape the surface scouring. As it brings us closer together, makes us all neighbors, destroys the old boundaries of identity marked out by national or regional consumption styles, we react by clinging to the margins of difference that remain. For fifty years, Yugoslavs spoke a common language, Serbo-Croatian, with a Cyrillic and a Latin orthography and minor regional variations in dialect, spelling, and pronunciation. In the descent into war, this common linguistic inheritance was fractured: Zagreb and Belgrade linguists began insisting that they spoke two languages, not one, and set out to purify each of its derivations from the other. Now, on the rare occasions when Zagreb and Belgrade intellectuals meet, they often prefer to speak in English.

Nationalism on this reading is not what Huntington would wish us to see: an eruption of ancient historical rivalries and antagonisms. It is a modern language game, invented to respond, as Ernest Gellner once said, to the uprootings of modernity. It meets these challenges to old identities by transforming identity into narcissism. It is a rhetoric that takes the facts of difference and turns them into a narrative justifying political self-determination. In the process of providing legitimacy for a political project—the attainment of statehood—it glorifies identity. It turns neighbors into strangers and the permeable boundaries of identity into impassable frontiers.

This is not to say that nationalism is always and everywhere a politics of fantasy. Just because the identity it validates may be a dubious concoction of invented traditions and modern paranoias does not mean that the identity in question is not really threatened. Nationalism does address the central problem of interethnic relations—inequalities of power—and insists that human beings cannot be at home with themselves unless they have self-determination. Moreover, nationalist language understands that people want to speak for themselves, rather than being spoken for. Where ethnic minorities have been subjected to genuine tyranny, where language and culture have been genuinely suppressed, national revivals, even nationalist uprisings, are both inevitable and justified.

The problem with nationalism is not the desire for self-determination itself, but the particular epistemological illusion that you can be at home, you can be understood, only among people like yourself. What is wrong with nationalism is not the desire to be master in your own house, but the conviction that only people like yourself deserve to be in the house.

This impulse is also driving the ethnic fragmentation observable in secure nation-states. Ethnic groups once content to accept assimilation on the terms dictated by the majority culture will no longer allow themselves to be spoken for. No one wants his voice to be taken for granted; no one wants her preferences aggregated into those of others. Blacks will not let themselves be spoken for by whites; women speak in their own voice; in Canada and Australia aboriginal groups demand the right to speak for themselves. Again, there is a good deal of alarm about these tendencies, much anxious talk about the ethnic fragmentation of multiethnic societies, particularly among the old elites who used to take for granted their right to speak and act on behalf of these minorities. Instead of fragmentation, we should think of this process as democratization: the fearful, yet positive logic of empowerment. The problem, however, is just who is being empowered—the individuals in these groups, or merely their spokesmen and leaders. Empowerment that *individuates,* that allows individual members of minority groups to articulate their own experience and secure respect from the majority, is one thing; empowerment that simply consolidates the hold of the group on the individual and that locks individuals in victimhood is another.

The problem with nationalism abroad and identity politics at home is *autism,* to use Hans Magnus Enzensberger's useful word: the pathology of groups so enclosed in their own circle of self-righteous victimhood, or so locked into their own myths or rituals of violence, that they can't listen, can't hear, can't learn from anybody outside themselves. What both nationalist consciousness abroad and some forms of ethnic consciousness at home have in common is the proposition that listening to strangers is worthless, since no one can actually understand you but your own group. What is denied is the possibility of empathy: that human understanding is capable of penetrating the bell jars of separate identities. But social peace anywhere depends for its survival on just such an epistemological act of faith: when it comes to political understanding, difference is always minor, comprehension is always possible. Once this conviction—this basic faith in the possibility of human communication as such—is lost, then politics becomes nothing more than an exercise in ethnic brokerage, in buying off discontent with patronage and various forms of positive discrimination. When a polity is broken up into ethnic clans who communicate only with each other in the language of collective threats and ultimata, it is on the brink of civil war. What prevents such a breakdown is not just trust but the kind of individualism that can survive only in conditions of trust: when individuals feel sufficiently free of fear that they do not need to depend exclusively on their ethnic, religious, or tribal groups to secure their basic interests.

VI

FREUD HIMSELF made the connection between nationalism, narcissism, and intolerance in his 1929 essay *Civilization and Its Discontents*. There he observes that "it is always possible to bind together a considerable number of people in love, so long as there are other people left over to receive the manifestations of their aggressiveness." Freud then went on to observe sardonically that his own people, the Jews, had "rendered the most useful services to the civilizations of the countries that have been their hosts," by providing them with a convenient target for all their suppressed hostilities. Freud's remarks about narcissism and intolerance were written on the eve of Hitler's coming to power. The following decade saw Freud himself and his family driven into exile. It cannot be accidental that it was an Austrian Jew who had such deep intuitions about narcissism and minor difference. No group identified more deeply with German *Kultur* than the Jews; no national minority was more successfully assimilated. None of this saved Freud or Austrian Jewry. No matter how assiduously they assimilated, no matter how carefully they eliminated the differences that separated them from their fellow citizens, the simple fact of being Jewish remained; that simple, surely minor fact (minor, that is, to the many Jews for whom it was a vestigial identity, one among many) Hitler turned into a major "biological" barrier between two races and cultures. As assimilation eliminated major elements of difference, minor vestiges acquired an increasingly neurotic salience among those, like Hitler, whose identities were threatened by Jewish assimilation. (It should be noted that while assimilation threatened anti-Semites, it also deceived the Jews, for it led them to confuse cultural and political assimilation. They were accepted in the concert halls, in the universities, and in professional circles. They failed to realize that cultural belonging did not confer political belonging.) In a remarkably short time Hitler succeeded in redescribing assimilation as pollution; once this was done, the absolute separation of Aryan and Jew was easily conceived as an act of purification. The language of purity and cleansing, so full of echoes today, is perhaps the most dangerous of all languages of narcissism. The distinction between cleanliness and dirt becomes the distinction between the human and the nonhuman, between the valued and the despised. The trajectory that begins with the narcissism of minor difference can end with utter moral abjection.

Let us pause here and draw some implications from what Freud is arguing. If intolerance and narcissism are connected, one immediate and practical conclusion might be this: We are likely to be more tolerant toward other identities only if we learn to like our own a little less. Breaking down stereotypical images of others is likely to work only if we also break down the fantastic elements in our own self-regard. The root of intolerance lies in our tendency to overvalue our own identities; by overvalue, I mean we insist that we have nothing in common, nothing to share. At the heart of this insistence lurks the fantasy of purity, of boundaries that can never be crossed.

VII

GENETIC RESEARCH SHOWS that there are no significant variations in the distribution of intelligence, of cognitive or moral ability, among racial, ethnic, or gender groups. The significant variations are among individuals *within* these groups. The paradox of intolerance is that it customarily fixes on the group differences as salient and ignores individual difference. Indeed, in most forms of intolerance, the individuality of the person who is despised is all but ignored. Intolerant people are uninterested in the individuals who compose despised groups; in fact, they hardly see "them" as individuals at all. What matters is the constitution of a primal opposition between "them" and "us." Individuality only complicates the picture, indeed makes prejudice more difficult to sustain, since it is at the individual level that empathy often subverts the primal group opposition. Intolerance, from this perspective, is a willed refusal to focus on individual difference, and a perverse insistence that individual identity be subsumed in the group. If intolerant groups are unable to perceive those they despise as individuals, it may be because intolerant groups are unable or unwilling to perceive themselves as such, either. The narcissism of minor difference is thus a leap into collective fantasy that enables threatened or anxious individuals to avoid the burden of thinking for themselves or even of thinking of themselves as individuals. Toleration depends, critically, on being able to individualize oneself and others, to be able to "see" oneself and others—or to put it another way, to be able to focus on "major" difference, which is individual, and to relativize "minor" difference, which is collective. What made that night in the Serbian farmhouse seem so suffocating was that ethnic war had nearly snuffed out these men's capacities to reason and reflect as individuals. I say "nearly" because in their confusion, one could sense them struggling to open up a space between what they felt and what the nationalist scripts told them to say.

VIII

IT MAY SOUND SMUG to talk about the Serbian reservists in this way, to suggest that they are in the grip of murderous fictions to which I and people like me are immune. In fact, what was most disturbing, in retrospect, about that night in the farmhouse is how difficult it was to defend, at least to those men, the nonmurderous fictions upon which *my* political convictions depend. For liberal beliefs depend on fictions no less than nationalistic ones. Behind those "self-evident" liberal truths—that all human beings are equal, that their persons should be inviolable, and that they have enforceable rights by the simple fact of being human beings—lies a fiction that the men in the farmhouse would have thought fatuous in the extreme: that human difference *is* minor, that we *are* brothers and sisters under the skin.

This is a fiction in the sense that it requires a self-conscious screening-out of certain empirical realities in the name of moral convention. For example, when defendants appear in a courtroom, judge and jury are supposed to ignore their visible identities—as men, women, black, white, rich, poor—and construe them as if they were simple, equal units of one indivisible humanity. All liberal institutions depend for their continuance on this complex and historically novel thought experiment. It is complex because it is so abstract: we are asked to deny plain facts and look beneath them to some elementary essence we all supposedly have in common. And it is historically novel: no human society has ever tried so assiduously to ignore difference in favor of commonality, and even we have begun to do it only in this century.

This historically novel process of abstraction makes a major statement about identity. It says: We are first and foremost juridical subjects, first and foremost citizens, equally entitled to a range of practices and protections; all differences are minor, and if they confer advantage, should be strenuously opposed. Needless to say, our "minor" differences do continue to confer advantage and disadvantage, and juridical and social equality remain far apart. But we are formally committed—and the institutions of our society depend for their legitimacy on this commitment—to the notion that difference should not matter. Without this process of abstraction and the institutions that practice it, we *would* be a tribal society.

In order to seize the singularity of the way we live, it is worth looking back at how we arrived at this sustaining fiction. The first steps toward imagining this abstract, rights-bearing creature occurred during the wars of religion in the sixteenth century. The problem was simple and drastically modern: Now that the confessional unity of Christendom had been broken, now that human beings no longer shared common religious doctrine, how could they be persuaded to trust each other and to live together in peace? How could they be persuaded to cease persecuting each other in the name of ultimate truth? The breakup of Christendom gave enormous impetus to the attempt to understand the basis of social unity. Once difference—in this case of a religious kind—had fissured the unity of a polity, what could possibly hold it together? The answer came slowly: economic interest and a commitment by each to certain prudential rules necessary to the preservation of all. From Hobbes through Locke and Adam Smith, the theory of society as an order of free individuals uniting to guarantee each other security, liberty, and prosperity began to take shape. The important, and often overlooked, point of this story is that these liberal theorists radically simplified the starting assumptions, simply took it for granted that the only conceivably free individuals were white, propertied Christian males. In this specific sense, the theory was a fiction, since it invented a community, not by reference to the actual populations of the time—which included women, children, nonwhites, and non-Christians—but by a process of tacit, unexamined exclusion. Initially, the only difference liberal theory sought to include was confessional. Even here, though, the range of acceptable difference was narrow indeed. Locke, for example, thought it inconceivable that political society could hold together if there were atheists or Muslims in the population. How could such persons, he asked, be counted on to observe the oaths that most men swore upon their Bibles? The doctrine of toleration that he elaborated in the 1690s thus applied only to Christian believers, to those who started with the shared premise of Christian revelation, however much they might subsequently disagree about doctrine.

Similarly, when the Founding Fathers of the new American republic set out to conceive a new state, they worked with equally constrained assumptions about difference. They restricted their community to white, propertied Christian males, and this in a society that included slaves. Such blindness is often held against the Founding Fathers and especially against that slaveholding liberal, Thomas Jefferson. Blindness it certainly was, and yet perhaps a necessary blindness. The liberal fiction might never have been conceived had it been required to include everyone: women, blacks, the propertyless, non-Christians, and adolescents. The liberal thought experiment would have been abandoned as a preposterous and even dangerous flight of fancy had political community been obliged to encompass all the observable human differences of late eighteenth-century society. Had liberal theorists not been able to take for granted the stabilizing impact of common ethnic, religious, and sexual origins in the composition of their polity, they would never have believed that such polities could cohere as systems of individual rights and interests. The civic compact they envisaged was conceivable only in the context of these shared assumptions.

We in the late twentieth century are the heirs of a universalizing language—one that speaks of all human beings enjoying the same rights—that was never *intended* to include all human beings. To argue that liberalism is a form of organized hypocrisy is to miss the point. Without such imaginative hypocrisy, it might never have imagined a society of equal individuals at all. And so the Founding Fathers did not dwell on the potential divisiveness of enshrining the rights of the individual. Rather, they assumed that each individual would be so embedded in the homogeneous group identity of similar class, race, and gender that no threat to social coherence could arise from the individualizing bias of rights language.

Once the liberal experiment began, however, its language of rights was picked up by every one of the groups who had been excluded from its terms. Again, instead of our dismissing liberalism as a system of hypocrisy, it is worth emphasizing the dynamic impact of the charge of hypocrisy upon liberalism itself. For once its terms entered the moral language, these terms could be turned, with scathing effect, on liberalism itself. Once the language of rights was enshrined in the American Constitution and the French Declaration of the Rights of Man and of the Citizen, it enjoyed a career that would have astonished its creators. Almost immediately, Mary Wollstonecraft raised the obvious question of how the word *Man* could be meant to apply to only half of the human race and how membership in the political community could be legitimately denied to creatures whose differences, in terms of reason, emotion, and moral intuition, were so decidedly minor. The argument over whether women should be included within the liberal polity raged throughout the nineteenth century and was finally settled—in favor of inclusion—after World War I.

First women, then the propertyless. The gradual enfranchisement of the working class and the abolition of property requirements for electoral participation occupied most of the political history of the nineteenth century. Again, as with women, the argument against their inclusion was that political community could not survive if class difference was incorporated and enfranchised, that stability and coherence depended on restricting difference, and so preventing its capacity to mobilize and therefore to destabilize. Again, as with women, the conclusive rejoinder was that political community could not survive *unless* difference was incorporated and enfranchised.

Incorporation had the effect of disaggregating difference, that is, of separating individual from group, giving individuals a conception of themselves as rights-bearing creatures with personal claims upon the state, and upon occasion, claims against the groups and collectivities—like unions—that had fought for their incorporation. As individuals gained political rights, the hold of collective identities like class and gender began to weaken. In this way, the incorporation of individuals into the liberal state acted to diminish the power of these forms of difference to define identity and divide society.

The next battle, and it has only begun since 1945, has been the incorporation and enfranchisement of racial difference. In the rhetoric of domestic civil rights and in anticolonial struggle for self-determination, the moral claim has been that a liberal language of universal human rights cannot, without contradiction, exclude any racial group. From Mahatma Gandhi, trained in the traditions of English common law, to Martin Luther King, raised in the language of radical Christian egalitarianism, leaders educated within but excluded from liberal society simply demanded what it could not logically refuse—that its moral terms apply to them as well.

The liberal ideal may be four hundred years old, but it is only within the last forty years, since the civic emancipation of non-white peoples, that we have actually begun the experiment in earnest—establishing a polity based on equal rights with the full incorporation of all available human differences. This is not to say that multiethnic, multicultural societies have not existed in the past—they have—but they have not been rights-based democracies. They have not been premised on a civic model of inclusion, on the idea that what holds a society together is not common religion, race, ethnicity, language, or culture, but common normative attachment to the rule of law and to the idea that we are all rights-bearing equals.

One effect of the explosion of ethnic war in the 1990s is to awaken liberal societies to the full magnitude of the task they have set themselves, to awaken them to the realization that for the first time in four centuries, they will actually have to live up to their starting premises or sunder into civil war. Whereas civic order traditionally depended on a variety of exclusions, now everyone is included, and the question of whether a genuinely "civic" order of individuals can flourish without depending on majority domination—in culture, language, religion, and morals—has acquired new urgency. Between 1945 and 1989, liberal society derived a great deal of its social cohesion from the existence of an external enemy. No longer. Now we have only Locke and Jefferson, and the words they left for us to live by.

Only now are we actually beginning to *live* by the words we purport to believe. First religion, then class and property, then gender, then race, and now age have all been progressively outlawed as grounds for withholding membership in liberal society. As we enter the era of the multicultural, multiethnic society we are constantly obliged to confront the liberal fiction: Do we treat X as a rights-bearing equal or as a member of a group? We know what we must do. Our moral language no longer allows us any excuses.

To be sure, none of us lives up to the ideal. Yet without this fiction—that human similarity is primary and difference is seondary—we are sunk. To ignore differences for purposes of political deliberation, moral behavior, and the rule of law is not to lie. But it does require us to see beneath the skin, a process that commits us to a unique daily exercise of the moral imagination. And this exercise of the imagination—this choice to focus on identity rather than difference—is what sustains liberal institutions.

This fiction also sustains a particular epistemology, which is at the root of tolerance as a social practice. The essential task in teaching "toleration" is to help people see themselves as individuals, and then to see others as such; that is, to make problematic that untaught, unexamined fusion of personal and group identity on which nationalist intolerance depends. For nationalist intolerance requires a process of abstraction in which actual, real individuals in all their specificity are depersonalized and turned into carriers of hated group characteristics.

To return to my starting point: Intolerance is a form of divided consciousness in which abstract, conceptual, ideological hatred vanquishes concrete, real, and individual moments of identification. My Serbian friend is at the edge of recognizing his enemies as individuals, only to succumb to the nationalist fantasy of their radical otherness. There is a consciousness, an anguish, an uncertainty, which could be fanned into something decent and human, if only he could read a newspaper or listen to a television broadcast that didn't poison him with hate and lies. If he had access to a public discourse—a newspaper, radio, television broadcast, political speech—that addressed him as a rational individual, he might have a chance of becoming one himself. To the degree that individuals can ever learn to think for themselves— and so become true individuals—they can free themselves, one by one, from the deadly dynamic of the narcissism of minor difference. In that sense, the function of liberal society is not merely to teach the noble fiction of human universality, but to create individuals, sufficiently robust in their own identity, to live by that fiction.

The Seductiveness of
Moral Disgust

I

THURSDAY, JULY 13, 1995: Boutros Boutros-Ghali's plane is heading south from Cairo, a small, cramped executive jet, a crush of luggage and people—his team of seven, plus three journalists. I have been called forward for a briefing. He is an intense, wiry, sallow-skinned man in his seventies, sitting alone in a window seat, looking out at the Sudanese desert. He wants to talk about Africa. I want to talk about Bosnia.

Srebrenica has just fallen. Dutch peacekeepers have been taken hostage. Women and children, after walking across the battle lines, have arrived in Tuzla; Bosnian Serb soldiers have captured all Muslim males between the ages of fifteen and fifty-five and led them away to unknown destinations. The United Nations' mission has been humiliated. Why doesn't the secretary-general cancel this trip, I ask, and fly back to the U.N.?

Because if I do, he says, all the African countries will tell the world that while there is genocide in Africa—a million people have died in Rwanda—the secretary-general pays attention only to a village in Europe. "Sre*bree*niska" is how he pronounces its name, in a low, raspy Levantine accent.

He once vowed to defend the "safe haven," but the Dutch, who have peacekeepers on the ground, vetoed further air strikes. Now the Office of the United Nations High Commissioner for Refugees is erecting a tent city in Tuzla, airfreighting food and hooking up water pipes—in effect, collaborating, yet again, in the ethnic cleansing of eastern Bosnia.

At least forty thousand soldiers were needed to mount a credible defense of the safe havens. Only seven thousand were made available by the member states. I cannot make out whether the secretary-general believes that, with so few resources, a defense was even possible.

Why call them safe havens if they were never safe? Why call UNPROFOR a protection force when it cannot protect itself? And why insist on being neutral, in the face of a clear aggressor and a clear victim, when that neutrality daily undermines the United Nations' moral credit?

"We are not able to intervene on one side. The mandate does not allow it," he says. He is vehement.

I wonder what kind of alibi this is. A secretary-general has little power, but he does have moral authority. I'm on the plane to see what use he makes of it, and I happen to have chosen the week when that authority seems to be at its most compromised, when Bosnia risks becoming what Abyssinia was for the League of Nations: the foreign field where honor is lost beyond recall.

Nothing in Boutros-Ghali's robust good humor suggests that he regards the moment as darkly as I do. He's had worse weeks. He is philosophical about his moral authority: it is by definition a wasting asset. Look, he says, we are negotiators. Nobody likes negotiators: parties to any dispute always find it convenient to blame us for their own failings. If the United Nations has failed in Bosnia, he implies, it is because no one—not the Muslims or the Serbs or the great powers—has allowed it to do the job it is capable of doing; if the U.N. is still there, it is because the great powers believe that the alternatives would be worse.

The secretary-general taps a blue file on the table in front of him. It is full of of cables from Zagreb, Belgrade, New York. He has just gotten off the phone with his special envoy to Bosnia, Yasushi Akashi, and the U.N. mediator Thorvald Stoltenberg. The secretary-general is in touch.

He says, "If we had not been there, it would have been worse." The war has not spread to Macedonia or Kosovo, and 2.8 million refugees have been fed and clothed and sheltered. "We have to do our work under terrible emotional pressure," he says, "especially from the media. No one realizes how long it takes for people to come to their senses." Remember how long it took, he reminds me, before the Israelis and the P.L.O. finally sat down to talk peace?

All this is true, but it does not change the fact that promises were made to people in a village in Europe that should never have been made, because those who made them knew the promises could not be kept.

It may not matter greatly if this thought keeps the secretary-general awake at night, but I am curious to know if it does. He gives nothing away, of course. A man in his position cannot afford *états d'âme*. It is beside the point to ask about his moods. He keeps them to himself. One can assume only that years of diplomacy and a life as a patrician member of Egypt's Coptic minority have taught him self-containment. His is a heavily fortified personality. But then, unexpectedly, he confesses, "Everywhere we work, we are struggling against the culture of death."

Failure in Yugoslavia, such a phrase implies, is relative. If you think we have failed in Yugoslavia, he seems to be saying, look at the places where we have not been able to intervene: the culture of death stalks Afghanistan, Chechnya, Sri Lanka, Sierra Leone, and Liberia too, and we do nothing. He calls these "the orphaned conflicts"—the ones that the West, selective and promiscuous in its attention, happens to ignore in favor of that village in Europe.

Did I suppose that Srebrenica or Sarajevo was the first place the United Nations had failed? The secretary-general recalls the fate of Beirut. He had friends there—civilized and tolerant people, who believed in the same multicultural illusions as the people of Sarajevo. The West was content to watch that city tear itself apart. That was twenty years ago. Why should we assume that such a thing will not happen again? He wants me to understand that this is not cynicism, exactly—just a sober understanding of how things are. Besides, there are places worse than Sarajevo, worse than Srebrenica, and he is going to take me to a few of them.

FRIDAY, JULY 14: Nyarubuye, Rwanda. One by one, four white United Nations helicopters appear over the banana trees and settle down on a burned-grass circle at the center of a Catholic missionary compound. Two bodyguards with AK-47s fan out beneath the rotor blades of the secretary-general's helicopter, followed by a third bodyguard with Boutros Ghali's flak jacket wrapped inside an overcoat. Huddled against low brick buildings stand a cluster of barefoot villagers, their faces gray with the dust kicked up by the helicopters. Some are holding up plywood placards stenciled in English. One placard reads WHERE

WAS THE U.N. BEFORE THE GENOCIDE? The secretary-general steps down from the helicopter and walks past them, his head bent.

The Hutu militia known as the Interahamwe ("We who strike together") arrived at this Catholic mission community in April 1994. They then separated the Hutus from the Tutsis and systematically slaughtered the Tutsis. Tutsis were hacked to death while cowering behind the pews of the church or under the desks in the classrooms, or while hiding in the swamp in the valley below, or while climbing into the trees. When the militia grew tired of killing, they immobilized their victims by slicing the tendons of their arms and legs, went off to rest, and returned later to finish the job.

When the Rwanda Patriotic Front, the Tutsi bush army, retook the area in May, the survivors returned from hiding in Tanzania. They then made a decision so astonishing that it was at first hard to credit. They decided to leave the corpses—in the thousands—where they lay: between the church pews, beneath the school desks, in the yard outside. The survivors turned the church compound at Nyarubuye into the Yad Vashem of African genocide.

The secretary-general is led to the doorway of a long, low room that was once used for Bible study. Stretched out on the floor are row upon row of dust-covered skeletons in rags. A dirty light slants across femurs, ankles, hipbones, shoulder joints, teeth, skulls. No flesh remains. There is no smell of putrefaction. The clothing has faded to the color of ash.

Boutros-Ghali is taken to an impromptu memorial, a small tin shed the size of a phone booth, where someone has swept together a pile of bones, fragments of cloth, and dry grass. His guards hand him a wreath, and he places it on this little heap. He stands for a minute and is photographed. He bows, shuts his eyes, then moves away.

He is led up a red dirt road to the latrines, where, even today, more than a year after the killing, the survivors are still digging out corpses. The secretary-general peers into the stinking darkness, then steps away to draw breath. The expression on his face is of a man withdrawing as deep into himself as he can.

At the foot of the church steps, survivors sit in the dirt awaiting the secretary-general. There are about a hundred, their faces upturned, silent. They may not know exactly who a secretary-general is, but they know what he is doing: in any language, it is penance. When the massacres began, there was a substantial Belgian United Nations detachment in Rwanda. At the time, Hutu radio broadcasts from Kigali incited the Interahamwe to genocide; the detachment could have shut down the radio stations. Machete-toting gangs roamed the streets; U.N. tanks could have stopped them. But action of this sort was, in the language of the United Nations, "beyond the mandate." Then, in April 1994, ten peacekeepers were tortured and killed, and the Belgian detachment withdrew. U.N. soldiers remained and protected those who took shelter with them, but they were unable to stop the slaughter beyond their gates. And now, a year later, the United Nations feeds and clothes the Hutu Interahamwe—across the border in Zaire, in the refugee camps of Goma.

When the secretary-general talks to the survivors gathered at his feet, he admits that he has failed them. He says that he appealed to dozens of countries to send contingents to stop the genocide and no one responded until it was too late. Even so, he tells them that "the international community" has not forgotten them. He promises that the guilty ones will not escape. They will be rounded up in Zaire, Uganda, and Tanzania, and they will be punished. The survivors listen, but it is only when they hear one particular sentence translated that they applaud: "They will be punished."

After the helicopter lifts away the secretary-general, I remain behind and listen to the survivors talking among themselves. At least he came, one says, and he expressed sorrow. Yes, that is true, someone else says, but he did not listen. He did not ask any of the survivors to speak. They know the murderers' names. They were once neighbors, even friends. The survivors need justice now, as much as they need bread, and they do not believe they will get it. And those untranslated words of consolation the old man had shouted—*Courage! Courage! Courage!*—before he walked away to the helicopter: they were French for something, but nobody knows what they mean.

SATURDAY, JULY 15: Luanda, Angola. From Rwanda, the secretary-general's executive jet flies three hours west and south to Angola. The United Nations is monitoring a cease-fire that it brokered last year between Jonas Savimbi's UNITA guerrilla army and President Jose Eduardo Dos Santos's government forces. In the annals of modern senselessness, Angola's civil war ranks as among the most savage. Well over half a million people died. Such a civil war could not have been sustained by its participants alone. The Americans and the South Africans backed Savimbi, and the Russians and the Cubans backed Dos Santos. In twenty years of intermittent warfare, these two sides turned a huge oil-rich ex-colony of Portugal, with enormous undeveloped potential, into one of Africa's more devastated wastelands.

In front of the Meridien Presidente Hotel, where the secretary-general is staying, a small posse of amputee children scrabble about in the dirty square. One child has fashioned a crutch from a chair leg; another, who has no legs, drags his body along with his hands. They fight to hold on to their pitch: outside the Meridien Presidente, there are always U.N. shoes to shine and the hubcaps of U.N. Land Cruisers to polish.

In Angola, now that both sides have destroyed the place they were fighting to rule, they have accepted a deal, and the United Nations has arrived, seven thousand strong, to keep that deal from coming unstuck. The U.N. needs Angola. After Bosnia, after Somalia, after Rwanda, the U.N. needs a success, and it is already claiming that it has achieved one here. But can it be a success at such a price?

Angola tells you a lot about what has happened to the United Nations since this secretary-general took over, in 1992. Then, there were four thousand peacekeepers worldwide; now, a mere three years later, there are more than seventy thousand. Wherever the secretary-general goes, he commands assets on the ground that most heads of state would envy: tanks, troops, helicopters, Land Cruisers, satellite dishes, convoys of trucks.

Twenty years ago, the Office of the United Nations High Commissioner for Refugees consisted of some lawyers in Geneva revising and amending the international conventions concerning refugees. Now it is a global rapid-reaction force capable of putting fifty thousand tents into an airfield anywhere within twenty-four hours, or feeding a million refugees in Zaire. Forty years ago, the World Food Program did not exist. Now it is capable of sustaining the populations of whole countries. The United Nations has become the West's mercy mission to the flotsam of failed states left behind by the ebb tide of empire.

The United Nations once oversaw discrete development projects. Now it takes over the political and administrative infrastructure of entire nations and rebuilds them from scratch. Angola is the latest laboratory experiment in the rebuilding of failed states, after Mozambique, El Salvador, Haiti, Namibia, and Cambodia. Through the desolate, garbage-strewn avenues of Luanda, well-paid civil servants from a dozen countries rush from meeting to meeting in white Land Cruisers. These lords of poverty talk the jargon of development: building "local capacity," strengthening "indigenous initiative." But there is an imperial premise at work here: Wealthy strangers are taking upon themselves the right to rule over those too poor, too conflict-ridden, to rule themselves. If it is an imperialism, is it benign? Only if it succeeds: if Angola learns to rule itself, and these well-paid agents of the international conscience do themselves out of a job. But no one knows whether it will succeed.

And the omens are not auspicious. Cease-fire violations are multiplying. Military chiefs have already set themselves up as local warlords. Although roads are demined by day, they are often remined at night. Few refugees have returned home. *Momentum* is a favorite word of Boutros-Ghali's. He is here to get some momentum started again.

At the end of a round of talks, President Dos Santos offers the secretary-general the presidential 707 to fly up to meet Savimbi, the president's archenemy, in his highland stronghold of Bailundo. On the way there, Boutros-Ghali invites the press into the 707's executive lounge, with its blue leather swivel chairs, liquor cabinet, and conference table. The splendor confirms the general rule that the more miserable the country, the more luxurious its presidential jet.

But Angola is not on everyone's mind as we fly to meet Savimbi. The British have convened a conference in London to decide the Western military response to the fall of Srebrenica. The Americans are talking about "disproportionate" air strikes directed at Bosnian Serb command-and-control. They want to take approval of air strikes out of the hands of the secretary-general. He is resisting. If he loses his veto power, he will lose the leverage he still has to manage the military and diplomatic response to the crisis. I ask him if he is feeling marginalized by the turn of events. "Not at all." Is he dismayed by the increasing disarray among the Western powers? He makes a wry face. "The disagreement is now more in the open."

I ask him how he reacts when he sees the Americans, the French, and the British attempting to intimidate the Serbs with threats of air strikes and then, a moment later, talking of withdrawal. He won't speak ill of member states in public, yet it is obvious from his manner that the frantic talk of withdrawal has taxed his patience.

"Withdraw from what?" he asks. To withdraw from Srebrenica or Zepa is one thing, but to withdraw from Sarajevo is to withdraw from Bosnia altogether. And if you withdraw from Bosnia, do you also withdraw from Croatia and Macedonia? And if you withdraw, who will bring the parties to the negotiating table? "I am looking for answers to these questions," he says, and he taps the blue Yugoslav file.

The presidential jet lands at Huambo, and the party switches to Beechcrafts for a thirty-minute flight to Savimbi's red dirt runway at Bailundo. As we touch down, teenage guerrillas festooned with shiny bullet bandoliers peer out from mud shacks amid the banana trees. As the dust cloud settles behind our Beechcraft, a big man in a night-club bouncer's white jacket and black shirt and sporting an eagle-topped cane walks over to embrace the secretary-general. It is Savimbi. They drive off together in a black Mercedes. Stuck on the dashboard is a Savimbi totem: a large, brown-and-white striped plastic dog. Its head bobs up and down as the limousine pulls away from the landing strip.

Later, in the photo call, held in a lugubrious strawberry-pink basement in a ragged strip of buildings that passes for downtown Bailundo, Boutros-Ghali pats Savimbi's hand and calls him "my dear old friend." This is a curious phrase, for United Nations resolutions on Angola have laid a large portion of the blame for the carnage that overtook Angola after 1992 squarely on the shoulders of the dear old friend.

Later, I ask Boutros-Ghali why the mantle of the secretary-general's approval has to be cast on such shoulders as Savimbi's. He gives me a mocking glance, as if to say that my scruples are beside the point: the family of nations is run largely by men with blood on their hands. Besides, the peace process in Angola is behind schedule. One massacre at a crossroads could start the madness up again. There are people in Savimbi's camp who want to return to the bush and fight. The rewards for cooperation with the peace process need to be spelled out. Savimbi must be stroked.

At the press conference, after the stroking is concluded, Boutros-Ghali catches sight of a banner at the back of the room that reads TRUE PEACE IS THE ONE IN THE HEARTS OF MEN. There *is* peace in the hearts of men, the secretary-general purrs as he places his arm around Savimbi. The journalists in the back of the room roll their eyes. Back on the plane, Boutros-Ghali shrugs, smiles his knowing smile. You have to encourage people. You have to make people believe, yes, that there is peace in their hearts.

SUNDAY, JULY 16: Gbadolite, Zaire. After Angola, Boutros-Ghali's plane crosses central Africa and touches down in the heart of the equatorial forests of Zaire. President Mobutu wishes a tête-à-tête.

But the president, we are told, is still at Mass. So we cool our heels in his guest palace, a suburban bungalow in a heavily guarded compound in the middle of the forest. Boutros-Ghali walks about, looks at his watch, runs his hands over Mobutu's collection of gold African figurines on their cool white marble plinths. CNN is airing its news summary on a giant color screen in the corner: Zepa has come under attack; the Ukrainian U.N. contingent's bunker is surrounded. Boutros-Ghali watches, his face emptied of all expression. Then he gets up and—the only moment when I see him step out of character—says, "This is globalization," as if he too appreciated the sudden weirdness of watching a CNN account of the fall of another European village, here in the jungles of Zaire.

Ten minutes pass. Then twenty minutes. Why are we kept waiting? I ask one of the secretary-general's aides. Because, he whispers, Mobutu is king.

A stretch Cadillac eventually draws up outside. It whisks the secretary-general away—we follow in a bus—and past the mud huts of Mobutu's villagers to a marble mansion on a mountaintop. Musical fountains are playing on a granite esplanade in front of the house, and we are invited to admire an uninterrupted 180-degree panorama of the steaming equatorial jungle stretched out before us. Suddenly, Mobutu is there in person, in a cream-colored business suit stretched tight at the seams. He is wearing thick-rimmed sunglasses and his leopard-skin hat. He leans his weight on a silver-topped cane. As he greets the women in the secretary-general's party, he murmurs, "*Enchanté, Madame,*" to each, and grazes the tops of their hands with his lips. Indoors, we are allowed to admire the gleaming gray marble floors, the Gobelin tapestries, the Louis XVI furniture, the Grundig television, the sparkling chandeliers, the industrial-size whiskey bottles in the drinks trolley. Then we are ushered out, and the tête-à-tête begins. It is whispered that Boutros-Ghali is trying to persuade Mobutu not to evict the Hutu refugees from Rwanda who have fled to Zaire in the hundreds of thousands.

When, forty-five minutes later, we are invited back in, Mobutu draws over two big men in suits and, as he squeezes

Boutros-Ghali's arm, says that these men, his ministers, will stand witness to what he has promised. Then an amusing thought occurs to him. He could always have them shot, in which case no one would ever remember his promise. But then, he says, with a wide grin at the secretary-general, "you might make difficulties about human rights." The faces of the ministers are set in the rictus of courtiers, while Boutros-Ghali allows himself a thin smile.

This is the job, I think, and if you are secretary-general, you make the following calculation: Mobutu is bad, but Zaire without Mobutu will be worse; for thirty years, the dictator has held power because Washington, Moscow, Paris, and London all make the same calculation. The dictator takes his international support for granted; this makes him a trifle careless about keeping promises. Three weeks after apparently promising the secretary-general he will not evict the refugees, his troops begin doing so and are captured on the evening news, striding through the camps driving women and children out with whips.

MONDAY, JULY 17: Bujumbura, Burundi. The tour is in its fifth day, and the only one who doesn't look exhausted is the briskly energetic seventy-two-year-old at the center of it. I never see him relaxing—I've never seen his tie loosened—and this morning he appears, bursting from an elevator, with his stooped and slightly hunched gait. The members of his entourage behind him are drained: you can see them in the corridors of the Hôtel Source du Nil, long after midnight, in their dressing gowns, taking cables into his rooms, fielding calls from New York, their beds strewn with papers. He drives them hard. His American security guard, an ex-policeman from Darien, Connecticut, recalls the days with Pérez de Cuéllar or Waldheim, when there was time for sightseeing on the tours. "Not with this one," he sighs. "When he looks down the schedule and spots a visit to the zoo, out it goes. In goes another meeting."

Burundi is one of those small, forgettable places that earn the international community's attention because of their propensity for self-destruction. Boutros-Ghali has flown into Bujumbura, a little town on the shores of Lake Tanganyika, in order to try to talk the Burundian political elite back to its senses. A Tutsi minority, long in power, and in control of the army, has been forced by the arrival of multiparty democracy to share power with the Hutu majority. A Hutu finally came to power as president in 1993, only to be assassinated. In the succession of massacres that followed, a hundred thousand people, Hutu and Tutsi alike, are thought to have died.

To stop Burundi from disintegrating, the secretary-general appointed a special representative, Ahmed Ould Abdallah, an indefatigable fifty-five-year-old Mauritanian diplomat, who bears himself with the imperiousness of a Saharan chieftain. In April 1994, on the night that the plane carrying the presidents of Rwanda and Burundi was shot down over Kigali airport, Abdallah went on radio and television to prevent false rumors from precipitating a bloodbath. He sat up all night with the army chief of staff, phoning the local commanders and ordering them to remain in barracks. Most observers credit Abdallah with saving Burundi from the genocidal frenzy that overtook Rwanda next door.

There are no peacekeepers in Burundi, and Abdallah doesn't want any. "What we need here is psychiatrists," he says. "I meet the politicians every day. They are all frightened of each other. When I shake their hands, they are dripping with sweat. There is not one who would not murder another for the sake of an hour of political power."

Abdallah is under no illusions: nearly two years of frantic work may have done nothing more than slow an inertial slide into the abyss. Three nights before, the sister of a Tutsi member of his own staff was ambushed by the Hutu militia on a highway south of the city, along with her army-officer husband. The husband was mutilated. The wife, eight months pregnant, was disemboweled.

The gangs that do these things are mostly in the pay of the local politicians. Abdallah has their phone numbers. From his heavily guarded residence, overlooking Lake Tanganyika, he calls them continually. "You must keep them busy, or they will get into mischief." What he says to the politicians is always the same: Take responsibility for what is happening; behave like adults; stop the reprisals; if you do not, you will end up being destroyed by what you unleash.

I go out with him on tour in his armored car through Bujumbura's ethnically cleansed neighborhoods to talk to the adolescents with the Kalashnikovs and grenades, who for the price of a few beers will firebomb a street. He gets out and confronts them, telling them that the cycle of murder and countermurder must stop, or they will all be swept away. No one seems to find it astonishing that a United Nations ambassador should be personally policing the wild zones of a small African city. But there is no one else with the resources or the credibility to do so. It is an experiment: preventive diplomacy as a way of stopping the spiral of interethnic killing. The U.N. could be doing this elsewhere, but it is short of people with the necessary toughness and charisma. Abdallah himself is due to leave Burundi soon.

I am invited to sit in on the process of preventive diplomacy at work. Boutros-Ghali is at the head of a baize table in his hotel and listens to the Hutu and Tutsi leadership, ranged on opposite sides, facing each other. The Hutus insist that the Tutsi-dominated army is waging a campaign of extermination; the Tutsis say that night attacks by Hutu extremists have rendered all constitutional dialogue impossible. The atmosphere in the room thickens with accusations, counteraccusations, stares, and contempt.

Boutros-Ghali says nothing until everyone has finished speaking. He then tells them that they make him ashamed to call himself an African. You seem to assume, he says, staring along the two rows of eyes that will not meet each other, that the international community will save you. You are deceived. Remember Beirut. Many good friends of mine died there, deceived by the same assumption. The international community is quite content to let you massacre each other to the last man. The donor community is fatigued. It is tired of having to save societies that seem incapable of saving themselves. He brings the flat of his palm down upon the baize table. "You are mature adults—*majeurs et vaccinés*," he says. "God helps those who help themselves. Your enemy is not each other but fear and cowardice. You must have the courage to accept compromises. That is what a political class is for. You must assume your responsibilities. If you don't, nobody will save you." He then sweeps up his papers and strides out.

Later that night, in the Hôtel Source du Nil, I ask him if he always adopts such caustic language in private.

"When I have to, yes." There is nothing personal about it. The anger is a professionally modulated set piece, designed to bring a craven, local elite to its senses.

Will it work?

"We are only the doctors," he says. "If the patient won't take the medicine, what can we do?"

The metaphor is not quite accurate. These patients aren't refusing the medicine. They are setting fire to the clinic. Is there a point at which they should be left to it—a point at which even a secretary-general succumbs to the seductiveness of moral disgust?

Everywhere he goes, he appears to be the prisoner of the expectations that these beggarly places have of the United Nations and of that exalted fiction, the international community. These expectations validate his organization: they are its real mandate, its raison d'être. And yet, in one way or another, he deliberately tries to reduce these expectations, to contain the inevitable disappointment and force people to rediscover their own capabilities.

I ask him if he is tired.

"Not at all. You see me as I am."

He recently said that the achievement of the United Nations' fifty years was to create a workable international system. I tell him that after five days on the road I don't see a workable international system; I see a jungle, kept at bay by desperate improvisation.

He shakes his head. It is not that bad. There is more reason to be hopeful. He is not discouraged. "We bring hope to the international community." And then he is gone, upstairs, meeting another militia leader with blood on his hands, taking another phone call from Akashi in Zagreb or the secretariat in New York.

Night settles on the Hôtel Source du Nil. The swimming pool is still. In the corridors, where his staff has been scurrying to and fro, there is silence, but it is soon broken by a round of gunfire and the sharp, concussive report of a grenade. Ethnic cleansing is under way half a mile from where the secretary-general is sleeping. Before I turn out the lights, I switch on CNN. There are unconfirmed reports from Zepa that Bosnian Serb soldiers have lured civilians out of hiding in the woods at the edge of town, lined them up, and shot them all. They say the Serbs were wearing blue helmets.

II

LOOKING BACK NOW, I can see that on the journey through Africa with Boutros-Ghali, I was witnessing the moment when liberal internationalism reached the end of its tether. The twin catastrophes of Srebrenica and Rwanda brought to a close a brief period of hope that had opened up in 1989. In the process, a historical opportunity was wasted. To see just what was possible, we need to go back to a comparable turning point. The Year Zero of 1945 led, in quick succession, to the founding of the U.N., the establishment of NATO, the Marshall Plan for the reconstruction of Europe, the Universal Declaration of Human Rights of 1948, and the revision of the Geneva Conventions and the laws of war. The years immediately following the collapse of the Soviet Union offered similar opportunities. The Soviet veto no longer paralyzed the United Nations; Soviet arms and advisers no longer sustained regimes and insurrections around the world. Instead of there being two competing human rights cultures in the world—one socialist, one capitalist—there was one set of minimum norms to which every regime in the world formally subscribed. It was not utopian to expect a new age of robust but pragmatic collaboration between the superpowers to damp down the proxy wars that were beggaring so many regions of Africa, Latin America, and Asia; it was not beyond the bounds of possibility to envisage, in the peace-dividend of the end of the Cold War, a sustained increase in aid and development budgets to the Third World.

These new opportunities were accompanied by a deep change in the moral atmosphere of international politics. The community of human rights and development activists, which had emerged since the early 1960s, had acquired domestic constituencies of support and sufficient institutional power to influence the foreign policies of major states. Organizations like the International Committee of the Red Cross, UNICEF, and the UNHCR became billion-dollar global operations and used newly globalized media like CNN to create a popular demand for international humanitarian interventions.

These organizations seized upon new facts about the modern world that have changed the very scope of the modern conscience. The media has broken down the compartments that used to restrict our moral concerns to our immediate family, neighborhood, province, or nation. Since the advent of television news in the 1960s, we have been brought face-to-face with human misery that was once beyond our ken and therefore beyond the ambit of those emotions—guilt, shame, outrage, remorse—that lead us to make other people's trouble our business. At the same time, the revolution in jet travel and the logistics of rapid deployment made us conscious, as we have never been before, that we *can* do something—and quickly—about the disasters we see on television. Finally, we are aware, as never before, of the sheer size of the stockpile of unused resources in the West—grain in our silos, dripfeeds in our medical warehouses, technological know-how in our engineers and doctors—that could be put to use in diminishing the horror of the world. These elements have changed the modern moral imagination: the boundaries of moral impingement are global and we *know* that we can make a difference. We have less plausible excuses for fatalism and inaction. The size of our capabilities, the volume of our unused resources, unite to accuse us.

The impact of this roused conscience on the foreign policy of nations was quickly apparent. In quick succession, the international community mandated one ambitious intervention after another: the U.N. operation to oversee elections in Cambodia; the Gulf War to reverse a dictator's conquest of a neighboring state; the international humanitarian attempt to rescue the Kurds and then create a safe haven for them under an American air umbrella; the intervention in Somalia to put down interfactional fighting and get food to famine victims; the dispatch of U.N. troops to Bosnia to protect humanitarian aid convoys. At the height of this wave of humanitarian internationalism, influential figures like France's Bernard Kouchner, formerly a founder of Médecins sans Frontières and a minister in President Mitterand's cabinet, proclaimed that the age of strict national sovereignty was over and a new era of intervention had begun. The U.N. resolutions that placed the Kurdish population under international humanitarian protection were seen as a key precedent in establishing the right of the international community to intervene in the domestic affairs of states when civilians were oppressed by local tyrants.

How long ago this all seems. As the century ends, the internationalism of the early 1990s resembles less the creative moment of 1945 than the failure of Wilsonian internationalism after World War I. When moral internationalism fails, isolationism returns, and the signs of a retreat are all around us. Since the Boutros-Ghali era, the number of peacekeepers deployed around the world has fallen, while the number of active wars has increased; the foreign aid budgets of major states have stagnated or declined; the media are shutting down their foreign bureaus. In the global village, we have returned to parish-pump politics.

As the moral activism of the early 1990s recedes, its historical contours become visible. It was intended as an attempt to put principle in place of realpolitik, to replace the old imperial language that had mandated intervention with a new language of humanitarian need. But ambitions, follies, and ironies of an imperial kind continued to haunt the operation. The dark jungles over which Boutros-Ghali's plane flew—and where we touched down briefly at Mobutu's retreat of Gbadolite—are close to the actual setting of the great fable of European imperialism at the end of its tether, Joseph Conrad's *Heart of Darkness*, published in 1900. In 1890, the young Conrad had traveled by steamer through the Congo and had been repelled by the sadistic savagery of some of the Belgian colonial agents in the region. These were the prototypes for Conrad's satanic Kurtz.

In *Heart of Darkness*, Conrad observed that imperialism, when looked at closely, is not a pretty thing. "What redeems it is the idea only." Kurtz's rapacious search for ivory was ennobled in his own eyes by his plans to bring civilization to the savages. In the end, of course, civilization redeemed nothing at all. When Marlow finds Kurtz, at the final bend of the river, all that remained of Kurtz's civilizing mission was a row of native heads stuck on pikes and the tattered remains of Kurtz's concluding report to the International Society for the Suppression of Savage Customs, on the final page of which the delirious Kurtz had scrawled, "Exterminate all the Brutes!" Conrad's work is a fable about late nineteenth-century imperialism paralyzed by futility and consumed by nihilistic rage. It is also about the seductions of moral disgust: having failed to civilize the savages, Kurtz turns against them all the force of his own moral self-disillusion.

The liberal interventions of the early 1990s were all avowedly and self-consciously postimperial. Yet they were haunted by

Conradian continuities and ironies. When Conrad symbolized imperial impotence in the image of the gunboat in *Heart of Darkness*, moored off the African shore, lobbing useless shells into the unanswering jungle, the contemporary imagination leaps to the image of NATO warplanes lobbing shells into abandoned Serbian artillery dugouts in 1994. Conrad himself could hardly have imagined a more telling image of imperial futility than the spectacle of U.N. soldiers, mostly Pakistani, firing upon Somali crowds and killing the women and children they were mandated to protect. Now of course all traces of the Somali operation have vanished, just as the remnants of the Belgian presence in the Congo are being reclaimed by the jungle. If, as expected, NATO troops are pulled out of Bosnia sometime in 1998, it might soon be the case that they might as well not have been there at all. Past and present meet in a shared image of the futility of great power.

The interventions undertaken since 1989 were seen as intentionally self-limiting and therefore moral exercises of power, uncontaminated by the lusts of empire. In Desert Storm, Allied troops were halted on the road to Baghdad: Saddam was allowed to remain in power, and we limited ourselves to an air umbrella to allow the Kurds to shape their future as best they could. In the case of Somalia, we precluded taking over the country for the sake of what was called a "quick exit" strategy. In Bosnia, a land kept in peace throughout the nineteenth century by either Austrian or Ottoman dragoons, we supposed until the summer of 1995 that the mere threat of our disapproval, trade embargo, and the occasional lob of a shell from our aircraft would make the recourse to dragoons of our own unnecessary. Thereafter, we supposed—with a naiveté that the old cynics who ran the Austro-Hungarian empire would have regarded as laughable—that we could put in our dragoons for a couple of years and then pull them out again, leaving Bosnia in peace. Had we been more ruthlessly imperial, we might have been a trifle more effective. If General Schwarzkopf had allowed himself to become the General MacArthur of a conquered Iraq, the Iraqi opposition abroad might now be rebuilding the country; if the Marines were still patrolling the streets of Mogadishu, the prospects of moving Somalia forward from the world of Hobbes to the world of Locke might be somewhat brighter; and if NATO had defended the Bosnian government with air strikes against the Serbian insurrection in April 1992, it is possible that Europe might not have had to witness the return of the concentration camp. Likewise, if after the Dayton peace accords of 1995, Western governments had simply taken over the administration of Bosnia, under U.N. mandate, at least until the local factions had given plausible evidence of being able to run their country themselves, Bosnia might have been reconstructed on a more secure foundation. The fact that such an option was never even a remote possibility suggests that a liberal interventionist foreign policy may be a contradiction in terms: principle commits us to intervene and yet forbids the imperial ruthlessness required to make intervention succeed.

In a postimperial age, we have forsworn imperial methods, but traces of imperial arrogance remain. What else could have led anyone to assume that any outside power could have gone into Somalia, put an end to factional fighting, and then exited, all within months? In Yugoslavia, it was not timidity that led us to avoid an early use of force, but arrogance that led policy makers to assume that stern words alone would bring cunning and ruthless demagogues to heel. We consistently overestimated our moral prestige and consistently underestimated the resolve of those bent upon ethnic war.

Moreover, when policy was driven by moral motives, it was often driven by narcissism. We intervened not only to save others, but to save ourselves, or rather an image of ourselves as defenders of universal decencies. We wanted to show that the West "meant" something. This imaginary West, this narcissistic image of ourselves, we believed was incarnated in the myth of a multiethnic, multiconfessional Bosnia. The desire to intervene may have caused us to rewrite the history of Bosnia to make it conform to our ideal of a redeemable place. Yet it was ironic, of course, that a Western Europe that had shown no qualms about ghettoizing its own Muslim *gastarbeiter* minorities suddenly discovered in Muslim-Christian coexistence in Bosnia the very image of its own multicultural illusions. Bosnia became a theater of displacement, in which political energies that might otherwise have been expended in defending multiethnic society at home were directed instead at defending mythic multiculturalism far away. Bosnia became the latest *bel espoir* of a generation that had tried ecology, socialism, and civil rights only to watch all these lose their romantic momentum.

While the intellectuals' moral outrage had a real impact on the outcome in Bosnia, it seems obvious in retrospect that the predominant motives for the American pressure that led to Dayton were political and geo-strategic rather than moral: America intervened to save the Clinton presidency with an appropriately timed display of global leadership, and, more fundamentally, to rescue NATO and the Atlantic Alliance. Since the refusal of the Americans to back Europe's Vance-Owen peace initiative in early 1993, Europe and America had been bitterly divided over Bosnia. Clinton intervened in Bosnia to preserve his alliances, and to do so on American terms. But Dayton is now a distant memory, and when our dragoons depart, the fighting may resume. As the

Austro-Hungarians could have told us, the Balkans have always laid bare the pathos of imperial power.

Very often in these liberal interventions the moral reflex— "something must be done"—was sustained by the unexamined assumption that we had the power to do anything. This assumption of omnipotence often stood between indignation and insight, between feeling strongly and knowing what it was possible to do. If we had started from more humble assumptions—that we can always do less than we would like, that we may be able to stop horror, but we cannot always prevent tragedy—we might have been more responsible and, just possibly, devised strategies of intervention that would have stood more of a chance of success.

Now that we are faced with the humbling and imperfect results of most interventions—low-level ethnic violence continues to be the likeliest future for Bosnia; Saddam Hussein remains in power; the warlords continue to bleed Somalia to death; the Great Lakes region of Africa continues to be sundered by the legacy of hatred left behind by the Rwandan genocide—there is an additional Conradian parallel to consider, the theme of moral disgust. It would be too much to say that "Exterminate all the brutes" is now the unavowed conclusion that many draw from Western failures. But many are already tempted by the related thought, "Let the brutes exterminate themselves."

In Burundi and Rwanda, the secretary-general's rhetoric was a hair's breadth away from such disillusion and disgust. And similar disillusion is felt elsewhere in the zones of danger throughout the developing world. In the civil wars that have laid waste to Sierra Leone and Liberia, in the twenty-year war that has left Afghanistan prostrate, the diminishing band of aid workers who struggle to deliver services to the wounded and displaced often feel, like the Conradian station chiefs in the Congo jungles, that they no longer understand why they are there at all. Moral disgust is more than a temptation; it is an objective reaction to events, to the year-by-year incapacity of elites and societies to help themselves. Compassion fatigue—on the part of the states and private donors who fund development—may be something more than tiredness. It may represent an active repugnance at the inability of societies that receive help to do anything to cure themselves.

This return of disillusion is furthered by the breakdown of the moral narratives that sustain engagement in the first place. By moral narrative, I mean nothing more than the stories we tell that make sense of distant places and explain why we should get involved in their plight. It is a fallacy to suppose that global media automatically create these narratives of engagement. There is nothing *in* the pictures of atrocity or suffering that automatically engenders compassion or involvement. Some pictures, some places engage us; others do not. Our moral engagements with far-away places are notoriously selective and partial. We are more likely to help people who look like us than people who don't; more likely to help people whose history or whose plight we can understand than people whose situation we cannot fathom. Our engagement depends critically on what narrative is provided for us by the mediators—the writers, journalists, politicians, eyewitnesses—who make the horror of the world available to us. What is noticeable is that the narratives on offer fall into two categories. The story of globalization tells us that the world is becoming one, and that countries that used to be beyond our reckoning altogether—the Asian tiger economies, for example—are fast becoming competitors. This narrative gives us reasons to engage with these countries and to consider them carefully, if only as potential rivals. The second narrative is the story of chaos. Robert Kaplan's famous article, "The Coming Anarchy," is perhaps the most influential purveyor of this theme. From his trips to West Africa and the Caucasus, he conjures up a narrative in which large zones of the world have been delivered up to anarchy, to forms of warfare so chaotic that it would dignify them to call them civil wars. They are wars of disintegration, between factions and bands, whose aims cannot be regarded even as political. They are fighting for drugs, for territory, for survival, and from the fighting there radiates nothing but more chaos.

If we put together the two narratives—globalization and chaos—it becomes apparent that we are not being offered a picture of the world that makes sense. At the very least, we have a fractured image: Tokyo, Singapore, Taipei, Paris, London, Rome, New York, Los Angeles are being wired together in a twenty-four-hour global trading economy. But vast sections of the world—central Africa, parts of Latin America, central Asia—are simply drifting out of the global economy altogether into a subrational zone of semipermanent violence.

This is not the place—even if it were in my power—to connect these two stories. The point is that the absence of narratives of explanation is eroding the ethics of engagement. When all we see beyond our borders is chaos, the temptations of disgust become irresistible. If we could see a pattern in the chaos, or a chance of bringing some order here or there, the rationale for intervention and long-term ethical engagement would become plausible again. We forget that the Cold War made sense of the world for us: it gave an apparent rationale to the wars of the Third World; it explained the sides; it identified whose side we should be on. We have lost our narrative, and with it, the rationale for engagement.

Our narratives, it must also be confessed, have escape clauses built into them. We require blameless victims, and when they fail to be sufficiently blameless, we cover our disillusion by holding them responsible. Why do we demand that victims should be blameless? The Kurdish political factions continued to feud with one another inside the haven provided by American air cover; when one group failed to get support from Washington, it turned to Baghdad, and the liberal interventionists who had supported their cause in 1991 then watched the edifying spectacle of Kurds leading Iraqi secret police agents to round up their Kurdish opponents within the enclave. Making alliances with the Kurdish people's worst enemy in order to settle scores within the Kurdish movement is certainly calculated to make Western friends of the Kurds proclaim, "A plague on all your houses." And yet what are a weak people to do, when they know that American policy has no serious commitment to their cause? If Bosnia returns to war, it will be easy for the West to disengage. After all, they "brought it upon themselves."

Blaming the victim is one of the temptations of disillusion. A very great deal of exculpatory moral disgust circulates around the failures of the new world order, a self-excusing sense that "we" tried and "they" failed. In fact, it is seductively apocalyptic to suppose *all* our actions were failures. The truth is more equivocal: Kurds *were* saved from extermination, but have no state of their own and continue to live on the sufferance of four malignant neighbors; the Somali famine was palliated, but the rule of the gunmen was not ended; Saddam was punished but not toppled; the West prevented the Bosnian Muslims from being wiped out, but did not prevent the dismemberment of their state.

Is this the best we could have done? Between those who now say we did as much as we could and those who believe we could have done much more, there has to lie a position where the ethics of commitment meets the ethics of responsibility, where the commitments we make to strangers in danger can be backed up by achievable strategies of rescue. If we can't find such a middle course, policy and public opinion are both likely to lurch continuously between the Scylla of hubristic overcommitment and the Charybdis of cynical disengagement.

To find this middle course, three questions should be considered: (1) When is it necessary for outside powers to use military force in civil wars? (2) When is it right to back a minority's claim to secede from a state? (3) How can civilian populations be protected from the consequences of civil wars?

The Vietnam experience exposed the decisive limitations that a democratic politics imposes on the use of postimperial force. Only in rare situations—Saddam's invasion of Kuwait—can democratic politicians succeed in creating the consensus that international military operations require. The electoral cycle guarantees that this consensus is bound to be fragile: in practice, only low-risk, and therefore low-gain, strategies of military intervention, based on airpower, seem to be practicable. The authoritarian populists of the Balkans displayed a shrewd recognition of this Achilles heel of modern postimperial power.

Yet the story of the Balkans seems to demonstrate that discriminate and targeted intervention—through airpower—is the only language that authoritarian populists understand. The isolated and embattled minority who called for military action to stop the Serbs as early as 1992 were proven right. The Dayton peace accords of 1995 became possible only when American airpower was used to shift the military balance on the ground. The second obvious lesson—from Macedonia—is that preventive deployment of troops by outside powers can prevent civil wars from starting. Small detachments can have a disproportionate impact. Since preventive deployments have been shown to work, the third lesson from Bosnia seems to be that if you are going to intervene, intervene as early as possible. An obvious corollary would be this: If you aren't prepared to intervene early, don't intervene at all. Half measures are usually worse than no measures at all.

The more difficult question is whether outside governments should encourage or restrain the breakup of states. In retrospect, Western governments should have informed the nationalist leaderships of the Balkans in the late 1980s that a peaceful dissolution of the Yugoslav federation was possible, but that any attempt to transfer populations or alter republic boundaries by force would be met with economic and military sanctions, including the use of selective air strikes. The problem, of course, is that until 1990, maintaining the unity of a federal Yugoslavia and the integrity of her borders appeared to be a better way to avoid nationalist war. European and American policy continued to proclaim support for a unitary Yugoslavia as late as June 1991. Unfortunately, Serbian authorities took such support as a tacit authorization to use force against the proclamation of Slovenian and Croatian independence. Even when war broke out, many Western governments continued to view the Yugoslav National Army's assault on Croatia as a federal state's legitimate response to a secessionist movement. The correct moment to shift Western policy is obvious only in hindsight.

The question about the legitimate use of force is thus necessarily connected to the question of when to back federal states and when to support their breakup. This problem will recur—in central Africa, in the Caucasus—wherever national minorities confront majority tyranny or injustice. Making the right choice depends on understanding the history of the region in question. If minority and majority have slaughtered each other in the recent past, it is unrealistic to expect them to live together in the future. A history of bad blood—of real and recurrent killing—does justify a claim to secession and self-determination if—and it is a critical rider—the territory claimed is defensible and economically viable; and if the seceding party is prepared to guarantee the minority rights of those who remain within their state. Conversely, in cases like Quebec, where there is no history of killing, it is hard to see how past injustice could justify the costs of separation to both sides. A distinct and recent memory of spilled blood is really the only criterion that justifies secession or international support for a minority's claims to self-determination.

The third question—how to protect civilians caught in the middle of civil wars—haunted the entire humanitarian effort in the former Yugoslavia. It is no disservice to the devotion and courage of the peacekeepers and relief workers who intervened on our behalf to ask whether, in the end, they didn't make things worse. We should ask, for example, whether the attempt to deliver humanitarian relief convoys to civilians in the midst of war zones did not, in the end, prolong the war. We sought, in principle, to bring relief to innocent civilian victims on all sides. Inevitably some victims were not so innocent, and inevitably much aid found its way into the hands of belligerents. The intervention strategy that was adopted, to protect the Muslims in safe havens, to keep Sarajevo from falling—while doing nothing to stop Serb bombardment—was perfectly consistent with the conviction that we could not commit ourselves to a land war in the Balkans against the Serbians. In effect, the West's policy consisted of saying this: We will not fight the chief aggressor, and we will not enable the victims to resist, but we will try to prevent the victims from being wiped out.

Yet by failing to stop and reverse Serbian aggression, the West became complicit in the destruction of Bosnia and its capital city.

The U.N. allowed itself to become the administrator of the Serbian siege of Sarajevo. The U.N. prevented the city from starving to death and yet, by doing nothing to break the siege, helped to prolong the city's suffering. Moral results could hardly be more ambiguous than this. The best one can say is that outside intervention prevented the creation of a Greater Serbia. Had Croatia not been recognized in late December 1991, it is possible that it would have been conquered entirely. Had U.N. detachments not gone into Sarajevo, it is possible the city would have fallen, and had it fallen, all of Bosnia would now be in the hands of the Bosnian Serbs. Western intervention, in effect, prevented the full realization of Serbian war aims. Yet the manner in which this was done should give us all pause. The strategies we chose made it impossible to adopt others that might have been more effective. By deploying peacekeepers on the ground, the West offered their lightly armed troops as potential hostages to local warlords, which, in turn, precluded sustained use of airpower. The delivery of humanitarian aid, necessary as it was, probably reduced the incentives of both sides to negotiate a settlement.

David Rieff and others have argued that the reason the U.N. failed in Bosnia was that it wanted peace, not justice. But this is precisely the aim of U.N. peacekeeping, not a sign of its failure. Peacekeepers, by definition, are impartial without being fair; it is not their task to make moral distinctions between aggressor and victim. Peacekeepers also, by their very presence on a demarcation line, effectively ratify the conquests of aggressors and impede attempts by victims to recapture lost ground. Peacekeepers, also by their presence, cannot look kindly on victims who fail to do the decent thing and give up fighting. Bosnian refusal to capitulate infuriated the UNPROFOR command who wanted peace at any price.

Journalists covering the war kept calling for U.N. troops to return hostile fire, to denounce and pursue the aggressor, and to call in air strikes, without specifying how the U.N., once engaged, could have avoided being cut to pieces by a determined Serb attack. Those who wanted a more activist stance from the U.N. did not appreciate just how vulnerable the U.N. forces were on the ground. The message of Somalia was that even the United States Marines could be humiliated when they shed their impartiality and set off in hot pursuit of a rogue warlord.

The U.N. stumbled toward a new form of operations in both Bosnia and Kurdistan: the safe haven. Throwing a cordon around unarmed civilians, while leaving their armies to fight it out, did at least address the problem of protecting civilians when a cease-fire is impossible. But a safe-havens policy is credible only on two conditions: if combatants inside the haven are disarmed, and if security on the perimeter and in the skies is sufficient to protect the enclave. Neither security guarantee was given in the case of Bosnian safe havens. The result was a ghastly charade in which the very phrase *safe haven* came to embody Western hypocrisy and impotence. The worst of it is that a decent idea—with potential application in other places—was disgraced. After Srebrenica, who will trust a Western offer of a "safe haven"? Yet finding a workable strategy to protect civilians in the war zones of imploding states is the challenge that will either make or break not just the U.N., but liberal humanitarian intervention in general.

The chief threat to international security in the post–Cold War world is the collapse of states, and the resulting collapse of the capacity of the civilian populations to feed and protect themselves, either against famine or interethnic warfare. In a world in which nations once capable of imperial burdens are no longer willing to shoulder them, it is inevitable that many of the states created by decolonization should prove unequal to the task of maintaining civil order. Such nations have achieved self-determination on the cruelest possible terms. Either they are torn apart by ethnic conflict, or they are simply too weak to overcome the poverty of their people. Former Yugoslavia belongs to a growing category of states, in the southern rim of the former Soviet empire and in Africa, that have collapsed, abandoning their citizens to the Hobbesian war of all against all, or some against some. What these societies need is internal peace followed by the construction of institutions in which the rule of law rather than the rule of the gun prevails. This is work that is totally ill suited to the post–Cold War style of instant intervention and quick exit. What is needed is long-term, unspectacular commitment to the rebuilding of society itself. Obviously, such work can be undertaken only by the people themselves, but an enduring commitment by outsiders can help.

In the nineteenth century, this work was "the white man's burden": Kurtz's burden, the building of the infrastructure of imperial rule and administration in infested and insalubrious jungles. In the Balkans, it was the work of the Ottomans, and then of the Austro-Hungarians. Shattered traces of their work still dot the landscape. At least in retrospect, imperial rule had a certain logic: Those who cannot agree to rule themselves may be able to submit to rule by strangers.

This logic did not survive the rise of nationalism and the doctrine of self-determination. We are now living with the consequences of the modern axiom that rule by strangers is worse than rule by your own; that it is better for people to govern themselves, even if they make a mess of it, than to be ruled by foreigners, even if these foreigners do a passable job. For democrats, there is no return from the truth of these axioms. Conrad was right about the deep ugliness of empire. There is no point in nostalgia for an imperial division of the globe. Yet the question remains, What is to be done when self-determination fails, when civil war or famine destroys a polity? Once the immediate crisis has been solved, who is to rebuild civil society? Who is to re-create the institutions necessary for self-determination to function? Even if some form of peace or permanent truce can be brokered in the Balkans, it will take a generation or two to rebuild the institutions on which civic trust and a functioning polity depend. Who is ready to shoulder this burden? There is no shortage of non-governmental organizations ready to take up the challenge: groups of lawyers prepared to go out and instruct people in the humble realities of civil and criminal codes; police to teach about law enforcement in multiethnic communities; doctors and nurses to rebuild health-care facilities. But the persistent weakness of these states—their incapacity to restrain and control violence—means that most of this well-meaning humanitarian internationalism drains away in the sand. What these places need most is states, and in a postimperial age, this is the one thing that outsiders cannot give them.

There has been talk of reviving the old League of Nations idea of trusteeships, turning whole states over to the United Nations administrators, not for months but for years, until ordinary people can shake off the fear and loathing that divide them. But it is doubtful that the international community has the staying power for such an exercise or that indigenous populations can endure being ruled by strangers. Over the long term, trusteeship is bound to engender the same resentments that led to uprisings against imperial rule, and at the end of the day, trusteeship may leave failed states as divided as they were when they went in.

If one stands back and surveys our fumbled and ambiguous interventions from the standpoint of Conradian irony, what is striking is the fragility of the moral bonds that connect the developed and developing world. Conrad's fable reminds us just how vile imperial rule could actually be. Yet it seems evident that empire and imperial rivalry provided the zones of safety in which we live with a permanent rationale for involvement in the zones of danger. With the passage of empire the developed "northern" world seems to have less and less reason to be concerned with the fate of the unstable, collapsing states and nations on its periphery. What is striking is the sense that our securities and our fates are all too divisible. The two narratives of the late 1990s—globalization and chaos—do not connect. Not even the nexus of economic interest is likely to link a developed world, whose dominance is based on knowledge, to a peripheral world, whose only offering is unskilled labor and raw materials. The rhetoric of the global village, the globalization of media, conceals this increasing dissociation between our most basic interests. Now it is not even clear that we need the ivory that lured Kurtz into the jungle.

This is the context in which the revolution in humanitarian concern should be seen. For there has been such a revolution: the refurbishment of the Enlightenment heritage of universal human rights, the emergence of vast constituencies of human rights activists, development workers, aid experts whose moral rationale is the indivisibility of human interests and needs in an interdependent world. Yet this struggle to assert humanitarian interdependence must struggle against rivers of history that seem to be running the other way: toward a disconnection between the economic and security interests of the developed and the underdeveloped portions of the globe. The Conradian irony is that this interdependence was more apparent to the Kurtz figures of the nineteenth century than it is to the postimperial politicians and businessmen of the late twentieth century. What needs to be understood more clearly—however pessimistic the implications—is that when conscience is the only linkage between rich and poor, North and South, zones of safety and zones of danger, it is a weak link indeed. If the cause of Bosnia failed to arouse the universal outrage and anguish that the atrocity footage on our television screens led one to expect, it was not because those watching such images in the comfort of their living rooms lacked ordinary human pity. The charitable response was quite strong. The real impediment to sustained solidarity ran deeper: in some deeply ingrained feeling that "their" security and "ours" are indeed divisible; that their fate and ours are indeed severed, by history, fortune, and good luck; and that if we owe them our pity, we do not share their fate. Most of us persist in the belief that while the fires far away are terrible things, we can keep them from our doors, and that while they may consume the roofs of our neighbors, the sparks will never leap to our own.

The Warrior's Honor

I

ON JUNE 24, 1859, a wealthy Genevan named Jean-Henri Dunant, traveling in northern Italy, watched from the heights around Castiglione while the armies of Emperor Napoleon III of France and Emperor Franz Josef of Austria fought each other in the vineyards and ravines of Solferino. All day, Dunant listened as the convulsive sounds of battle rose through clouds of dust and cannon smoke. At dusk, the emperor of Austria abandoned the field, and his troops streamed away in defeat. Stendhal, in *The Charterhouse of Parma,* had described the confusion of battle at Waterloo; Tolstoy, in his *Sevastopol Stories,* had described the camaraderie of the Russian redoubts of the Crimean War. But there is no account more unsparing than Dunant's *A Memory of Solferino* of what a battlefield looks like after a battle: the earth black with congealed blood and littered with abandoned guns, packs, and tunics; everywhere severed body parts, splintered bone fragments, cartridge boxes; riderless horses nosing about among the corpses; faces twisted in the convulsions of death; wounded men crawling toward pools of bloody mud to slake their thirst; and avid Lombard peasants scurrying from corpse to corpse, to rip the boots from the feet of the dead.

Entering Castiglione, Dunant found several thousand wounded soldiers of both empires dying side by side in the churches, squares, and lanes of the village. Sending for medical dressings and other essential supplies, and enlisting village women, he set about tending the wounded, aided by a pair of passing English gentlemen on holiday. Dunant, then in his early thirties, was a rank amateur, a battlefield tourist. He had never nursed anyone in his life. Dressed in his increasingly bloodstained white linen suit, he wandered among the dead and dying, crammed into the nave of the village church, passing out cigars in the belief that the whiff of a good Havana would allay the stench of putrefying wounds. There was little but water to clean the wounds and some lint for field dressings. Ten hours of battle had claimed six thousand lives; in the months that followed, thousands more soldiers were to die from their injuries.

It is doubtful Dunant saved a single life that weekend. After only a few days, he gave up and returned to Geneva. But what he had seen was to change his life. For most liberal Europeans, Solferino was a glorious victory that helped to secure the eventual freedom of Italy from the Austrians. For Dunant, Solferino was a moral puzzle he was to struggle to decipher all his life, and the neglect of the wounded a scandal that gave the lie to myths of a nation's gratitude to its soldiers. He decided to write up his experiences and marshal the conscience of his time. When his *Memory* was published, in 1862, with its descriptions of the Castiglione nurses who said of their dying patients, *"Tutti fratelli"* ("They are all brothers"), the man in the bloodstained linen suit became a moral celebrity. He had seen something immemorial—the field of battle—and somehow seen it anew; paid attention, as few had before, to the wounded and dying left behind when the captains and kings departed. Like Florence Nightingale in the Crimean campaign, he had refused to accept that war was a matter for soldiers alone: as a civilian, he had strode into their moral sphere and insisted that what happened there was everyone's business. Nightingale had found rats in the Scutari hospital, soldiers without even a bed to die on, and she had shamed the British army into doing something. Dunant set out to do the same. He toured the capitals of Europe, using his fame to gather support for a new project—an international convention, which would allow for first-aid societies to care for the wounded in wartime. He wrote Florence Nightingale and sought to enlist the support of that hypochondriacal and reclusive saint, but she pointedly refused. She insisted that each country's army medical service should remain responsible for its wounded. Being Swiss, Dunant was in favor of an international organization of neutral volunteers to look after the wounded on both sides. A five-man committee of Genevan notables—the nucleus of what was to become the International Committee of the Red Cross, or the I.C.R.C.—was formed in February of 1863 to propagate Dunant's ideas.

In August of 1864, the Swiss government hosted in Geneva a meeting of representatives from sixteen countries, including the United States, to agree on improvements in medical services on the battlefield. During the meeting, one man suggested that medical workers wear a white armband; another proposed adding a red cross—as a tribute to the Swiss flag, with its white cross on a red background. The Red Cross—perhaps the most universally recognized symbol in the world—was born. Three weeks later, twelve of the representatives signed what became known as the Geneva Convention. The convention, the first of its kind, agreed to "neutralize" hospitals, ambulances, and medical staff, and it established the principle that enemy soldiers deserved the same medical treatment as troops of one's own nation. It did not fix any penalties for noncompliance, and it had no mechanism for enforcement, but it set a standard that combatants had to meet if they wished to be thought "civilized," and for Dunant that was enough. Even in Dunant's time, the idea of "civilizing" warfare seemed a paradoxical—even a perverse—notion. The American Civil War, which was being fought to a bloody conclusion as the Geneva Convention was being signed, was anything but civilized; anyone harboring illusions about the glories of war had only to view Mathew Brady's photographic images of the dead of Gettysburg, their pockets turned out by thieves, their feet bloated with putrefaction.

The first Geneva Convention dates from the moment when war was becoming both more savage and more visible. The first practical machine gun—the Gatling gun—was used in the Civil War and began the process, culminating at the Somme and Verdun, of the mechanization of slaughter. At the same time, the battlefield came closer to the reading public at home. Like Brady's photography, the invention of Morse code and telegraphy broke down the moral distance that had separated civilians from the realities of slaughter. The new technology created a new moral agent—the war correspondent—and a new moral genre—the war report—both of which from the 1860s onward helped to create the distinctive modern sense of dissonance between the myth of glory and its bloody reality.

The Geneva Convention should also be seen as an attempt to salvage the decencies of warfare practiced under the seventeenth- and eighteenth-century ancien régime from the new savagery introduced by Napoleonic mass conscription. The enormous cost of mercenary armies in the era of Louis XIV, for example, ensured that rulers had a strong incentive to reduce the wastage of men to wounds and disease. The royal hospitals at Chelsea and the Invalides in Paris, both of which date from the seventeenth century, and both of which were veterans' hospitals, attest to this solicitude. The democratic revolution of 1789 created the modern mass conscription army, and with the whole of the population to draw upon, Napoleon could afford to be profligate with the lives of his soldiers. Moreover, democratic war dispensed with the niceties observed when war was a tournament between aristocracies. The armies of the French kings were more likely to respect the neutrality of medical teams than the armies of the French republic, which went into battle with the belief that war was a contest between democracy and reaction, with no holds barred. In the first half of the nineteenth century, battlefield medical services were allowed to lag far behind innovation in logistics, technology, and tactics. A foot soldier thus stood a better chance of surviving a battlefield wound in 1690 than he did at Solferino.

One might have expected the age of democratic war to display a new solicitude toward the lives of the ordinary foot soldier and a concern that he be honored in death. In fact, at Waterloo, the common dead of both armies were left to rot on the battlefield; their bones were gathered up by English contractors, shipped back to Britain, ground up, and sold as bonemeal and fertilizer. It was only after the Crimean War and the American Civil War that the idea began to enter general currency that the dead deserved something better. Slowly the idea gained ground that each soldier, no matter what his rank, deserved the moral recognition of individual burial with his own headstone. The Geneva Convention of 1864 thus coincides with the beginnings of a complex revolution in the moral consideration afforded the wounded and the dead on the field of battle: an attempt to refurbish older military traditions of honor for a new age of democratic battle, and to extend the decencies of nurture and memorial beyond the aristocratic warrior elite to the common man, the new masters of the age.

It might be thought that this complex moral evolution occurred against the backdrop of a generalized revulsion toward war itself. But this was not the case. Dunant's encounter with the Solferino battlefield did not turn him into a pacifist. Part of the appeal of his *Memory* lay in a hardheaded acceptance of the inevitability of war, coupled with his admiring endorsement of the heroism of warrior culture—in, for example, a story he told of a French colonel who rallied his faltering troops at Solferino by seizing the regimental standard and crying, "Every man who loves this flag, follow me!" But Dunant also seems to have recognized that he was living between two ages: the age of chivalry and the new one of the machine gun—an "age when we hear so much of progress and civilization," he wrote, and yet one in which war could not be avoided. "Is it not a matter of urgency to prevent or at least to alleviate the horror of war?" he asked.

In August of 1870, when Bismarck's Prussia invaded France, Dunant's ideas faced their first test in battle. The International Committee in Geneva brought to the French government's attention the fact that few of the French soldiers appeared to know about the convention and few of their military nurses had been provided with the Red Cross armband. That fall, the committee intervened when the Prussians refused to hand over convalescent French soldiers, as the convention provided, because the French couldn't guarantee that they would not return to the front. Dunant proposed that Paris be declared a "safe haven," to protect its civilians from attack; his proposal was ignored. Paris came under siege, and the new Red Cross emblem flying above its hospitals was fired upon. By then, Dunant was in financial difficulties, and, when an Algerian business failed, he felt obliged to give up his post as secretary to the International Committee. He withdrew to a small town on the shore of Lake Constance. "I had learned what poverty meant for others," he wrote, "but now it has overtaken me." For twenty-three years, he lived in obscurity until he was rediscovered by an inquisitive journalist; in 1901, he was awarded the first Nobel Peace Prize. He gave the prize money away and died—irrepressibly hopeful to the last—at the age of eighty-two, in 1910.

By the time of Dunant's death, most countries had established national Red Cross societies. A Civil War nurse, Clara Barton, founded the American society in 1881. In the Muslim world the societies were, and still are, known as the Red Crescent. By the First World War, the Red Cross had become what it still is today, the largest humanitarian movement in the world.

In the field of international law, by the eve of 1914 the campaign to civilize war had spread a canopy of new conventions over the battlefield. As early as 1868, the Declaration of St. Petersburg banned "explosive" and "inflammable" projectiles and declared that "the only legitimate object which States should endeavor to accomplish during war is to weaken the military forces of the enemy." The Hague Convention of 1907, and the revision of the Geneva Convention in 1906, codified the law of war on land and sea, and laid down ground rules for the treatment of prisoners of war. The rule, for example, that prisoners under interrogation are required to reveal only their name, rank, and serial number dates to these conventions. While Europe furiously rearmed, it simultaneously sought to make war submit, in the words of one Hague Convention clause, to "the laws of humanity and the dictates of the public conscience." These conventions allowed Europe to believe, as it lurched toward Götterdämmerung, that if war came, it would conform to conventional rules and decencies. It is even possible that this illusion made war more likely, lulling people into trusting that moral rules could contain and control industrialized slaughter. By 1914, Dunant's idea of civilized warfare was a central element of European culture's self-regard, its complacent belief that civilization had vanquished barbarism once and for all.

A few critics registered dissent. The Prussian military theorist Carl von Clausewitz—writing in the 1820s, before Dunant's time—had dismissed the idea that war could be civilized by an international convention. "War is an act of force," he wrote, "to compel our enemy to do our will. . . . Attached to force are certain self-imposed, imperceptible limitations hardly worth mentioning, known as international law and custom, but they scarcely weaken it." But Clausewitz took it for granted that even total war was a rational ritual, a regulated use of violence to achieve political and diplomatic ends by other means. He also believed that violence ought to observe certain moral proprieties: His vision of total war did not include the indiscriminate slaughter of civilians or the murder and torture of prisoners. Such practices, he assumed, were beneath a soldier's dignity.

To be fair, Dunant himself never believed in the authority of an international convention alone. Without ever arguing the point, he understood that such conventions drew upon a deeper moral source—the codes of a warrior's honor. While these codes vary from culture to culture, they seem to exist in all cultures, and their common features are among the oldest artifacts of human morality: from the Christian code of chivalry to the Japanese Bushido, or "way of the warrior," the strict ethical code of the samurai, developed in feudal Japan and codified in the sixteenth century. As ethical systems, they were primarily concerned with establishing the rules of combat and defining the system of moral etiquette by which warriors judged themselves to be worthy of mutual respect. Warrior's honor implied an idea of war as a moral theater in which one displayed one's manly virtues in public. To fight with honor was to fight without fear, without hesitation, and, by implication, without duplicity. The codes acknowledged the moral paradox of combat: that those who fight each other bravely will be bound together in mutual respect; and that if they perish at each other's hand, they will be brothers in death.

Warrior's honor was both a code of belonging and an ethic of responsibility. Wherever the art of war was practiced, warriors distinguished between combatants and noncombatants, legitimate and illegitimate targets, moral and immoral weaponry, civilized and barbarous usage in the treatment of prisoners and of the wounded. Such codes may have been honored as often in the breach as in the observance, but without them war is not war—it is no more than slaughter.

Warrior codes were sharply particularist: that is, they applied only to certain people, not to others. The protections afforded by the chivalric code applied only to Christians. Toward infidels, a warrior could behave without restraint. The unique feature of the European natural law tradition, which began to take shape in the sixteenth century, as jurists struggled to find a way to reconcile the laws and customs of competing and often warring religions and states, was its universalizing ambition. Natural law, upon which the Geneva Convention was based, attempted, for the first time, to imagine rules that would apply to everyone, Christian and infidel, secular and believer, citizen and noncitizen.

The Geneva Convention both codified European warriors' honor and sought to make it universal, that is, to shed its particularist bias, to open its protections to everyone, regardless of whose flag they fought under. But law's dominion over war has always been uncertain. The decisive restraint on inhuman practice on the battlefield lies within the warrior himself, in his conception of what is honorable and dishonorable for a man to do with weapons. In the words of the British military historian John Keegan, "There is no substitute for honor as a medium of enforcing decency on the battlefield, never has been and never will be. There are no judges, more to the point, no policemen at the place where death is done in combat."

SOLFERINO WAS a one-day tournament between armies. At Verdun and at the Somme, war became a massed confrontation between societies. Dunant's ideals might well have died in Flanders's fields—along with so many other nineteenth-century notions of moral progress. But the surprising fact is that the First World War itself was the making of the modern Red Cross movement. National Red Cross societies on both sides of the conflict enlisted women—everyone from the czarina of Russia to the British housewife—into the war effort. Throughout the war, they rolled bandages, prepared food parcels for prisoners, managed hospitals, and nursed the sick. The International Committee of the Red Cross capitalized on Swiss neutrality to make itself an essential go-between on humanitarian questions. It expanded its mandate from care of the wounded to visiting thousands of prisoners of war on both sides of the front line. Its headquarters, in Geneva, became the clearinghouse for the millions of cards, letters, and parcels that families sent to their sons in confinement, and its Central Tracing Agency handled millions of requests to locate missing soldiers. Even though international law had not given the agency any explicit mandate to do so, it also passed messages between civilian noncombatants and helped families separated by war to be reunited. War was the making of the Red Cross, and it is at the heart of its complexity as an institution that war remains its reason for being.

To this day, neutrality remains the core of the International Committee of the Red Cross's moral politics. It makes no distinction between good wars and bad, between just and unjust causes, or even between aggressors and innocents. Its ethic is simple: to reach the victims wherever they are and to teach warriors to fight by the rules. But the doctrine of neutrality has become steadily more controversial as the new politics of human rights has entered the field. In 1948, the United Nations adopted the Universal Declaration of Human Rights, which said, in the ringing tones of its first article, "All human beings are born free and equal in dignity and rights. They are endowed with reason and conscience and should act towards one another in a spirit of brotherhood." Whatever "brotherhood" may mean, it cannot include making war. The modern human rights tradition sees war as a moral violation, and, between the war maker and his victim, human rights activists cannot remain neutral.

In 1949, the I.C.R.C. updated its charter, establishing four separate treaties, known as the Geneva Conventions. The conventions make no ringing claims about human brotherhood. Instead, they accept war as a normal anthropological ritual— the only way that certain human disputes can be resolved. They seek only to ensure that warriors conform to certain basic principles of humanity, the chief principle being to spare civilians and medical personnel. These two traditions—human rights and the laws of war—inspire humanitarian activists in all the world's danger zones, but they are in fact two different practical moralities. Even within the Red Cross itself, the conflict between these moralities remains unresolved. There are those who insist that the Red Cross's ultimate responsibility is to attack the causes of war, while others believe it is only there to tame the beast.

Most Americans may know the Red Cross only for its blood banks and for Elizabeth Dole. The American Red Cross is one of a hundred and seventy national societies, which deal mainly with their nations' domestic emergencies. It is the International Committee of the Red Cross that makes war—and the taming of war—its core business. Its headquarters, on a hillside overlooking Geneva, could easily be taken for a health spa or the head office of a drug company, were it not for the numbers of lean, intent young men and women in shirtsleeves and jeans urgently shuttling between buildings. The committee, composed mainly of Swiss lawyers, bankers, and diplomats, is presided over by Cornelio Sommaruga, a voluble but wily Italo-Swiss lawyer. When I once asked Sommaruga why an international organization should be run by a Swiss committee, he turned my question on its head: Only an executive composed of a single nationality—in this case, the Swiss—could be free of the paralysis that often afflicts multinational organizations, like the United Nations. These Swiss notables run what their rivals reluctantly concede is the most widely admired relief organization in the world. The I.C.R.C. employs about nine hundred expatriate field-workers (its "delegates") and seven thousand local staff and national-society members on an annual budget of $620 million. The organization is involved in as many as eighty countries, and works across the front lines of every armed conflict in the world, whether the media are there, as in Afghanistan, or are not, as in Sri Lanka or East Timor.

Although the national Red Cross societies depend mainly on private donations, the I.C.R.C. gets most of its money directly from governments. The Swiss government is the third-largest contributor, the European Union the second-largest. The biggest government donor is, surprisingly, the United States, which in 1995 contributed around $170 million. The size of the American contribution—from a country that owes the United Nations $1.6 billion and whose politicians seem regularly to revile international organizations—is a testimony to the I.C.R.C.'s legitimacy in Washington. In the Gulf War, the I.C.R.C. won General H. Norman Schwarzkopf's grudging respect for its supervision of prisoner exchanges and hostage releases; and when the organization takes positions that irritate the Americans—as it did when it insisted that General Manuel Noriega of Panama be allowed to receive visits in his Florida jail as a bona fide prisoner of war—it does so with characteristic discretion. Its hardheaded neutrality makes it a useful intermediary in tense and potentially violent political standoffs, like the siege of the Japanese Embassy residence in Lima, Peru, where the I.C.R.C. refused to act as a mediator, but helped to keep both sides talking, ferrying everything from heart medicines to fresh panty hose, to guerrillas and hostages alike.

The organization's attitude toward war is very Swiss. Despite almost two hundred years of peace and neutrality, Switzerland is not a pacifist culture. Its official doctrine is armed neutrality. Every Swiss receives some form of military training; hence many I.C.R.C. delegates know how to clean and assemble the weapons that are so often waved in their faces at checkpoints. It is not an accident that one of its most heroic delegates, Dr. Marcel Junod, who saw action as a humanitarian relief worker from the 1935–36 Abyssinian war to Hiroshima, entitled his memoirs *Warrior without Weapons*. There is a curious parallel between the I.C.R.C. culture and the military culture it shadows and tries to control. The I.C.R.C., like an army, respects discipline, order, and honor. It works best when it is face-to-face with warriors.

Until 1991, the organization's field staff was closed to non-Swiss, on the grounds that delegates of non-Swiss nationality might compromise its reputation for impartiality and neutrality. But in the past six years it has been recruiting other nationalities, has added English to French as its chief working languages, and is widening the distance between itself and its Swiss anchorage. Until ten years ago, the I.C.R.C. shut out the press. It used to pride itself, like the Swiss banks, on discretion and privacy. But, like the Swiss banks, it discovered that these virtues frequently arouse suspicion. Now it has press officers in most major delegations.

In the I.C.R.C. training course at Cartigny, outside Geneva, new delegates are taught how to drive through minefields, how to talk their way through checkpoints, and how to escape from their vehicles if they come under rocket attack. They are subjected to a mock hijacking, complete with masked men and with what trainees say is a realistic barrage of verbal and physical intimidation. They are told never to carry weapons in their vehicles or to allow fighters of any description to travel in them. And it is made clear to them that they depend for their security on the impalpable and uncertain moral authority of the Red Cross emblem and on their studiously maintained impartiality.

The I.C.R.C. delegates probably know more about modern war than any other group of people on earth, including most generals. Other humanitarian organizations usually withdraw or relocate their personnel when the shooting gets bad. The I.C.R.C. makes a point of staying in: all of its major delegations are equipped with bunkers, sandbags, and antiblast windows. Its delegates have seen modern war at its most primitive: in Rwanda, they watched through the windows of their vehicles while Interahamwe gangs roamed the streets of Kigali hacking civilians to death with machetes. They have also seen war at its most hightech: Swiss delegates who remained in Baghdad in January 1991 witnessed the awesome son et lumière of the Tomahawk cruise missiles.

Despite the risks, or perhaps because of them, the I.C.R.C. always has more applications from volunteers than it can accept. It takes on young graduates with degrees in international relations seeking a year or two of adventure before joining banks; ex-hippies with a longing to travel; former taxi drivers; doctors and nurses tired of the safe ways of Swiss clinics. All come in search of one of the most elusive things in the world—the intangible satisfaction of doing something worthwhile. In addition to preparing a "letter of motivation," a prospective delegate is put through a tough interview. One told me that the first question he was asked was "So what are you here to escape?" Sometimes it is a failed marriage, the claustrophobic security of Swiss life, or the featureless grind of a modern career. Most delegates start with illusions of changing the world; some burn out, and others continue, recompensed by the rewards of small deeds—reuniting members of a family separated by war, locating a prisoner thought to have been killed or to be missing in action.

From the First World War through the Hungarian uprising of 1956, the I.C.R.C. has been one of the most prominent players on this field of good deeds. Its relief workers were the first to reach the German concentration camps in 1945; one of its delegates was the first neutral observer to reach Hiroshima. But since the age of televised disaster, which began with the Biafran war of 1968, the field has become crowded with competitors, among them the United Nations agencies. National Red Cross societies have also been elbowing their way into the lucrative media world of war zones. Interagency competition for donors, headlines, and victims is now a vast, unruly humanitarian bazaar, and the I.C.R.C. is struggling to be heard above the din and to maintain its principles. Its doctrine of neutrality is called into question by organizations like Médecins sans Frontières, which maintains that humanitarian intervention cannot be impartial between the Serb militiaman and the Muslim civilian, or the machete-wielding Hutu and the Tutsi victim. The I.C.R.C.'s doctrine of discretion and silence—which allows it to work both sides of a conflict—is also criticized by journalists, on the grounds that its silence has shaded into complicity with war crimes. All this leaves the I.C.R.C. wondering whether Dunant's insistence that all victims are equal, whatever the justice of their cause, makes sense in the bitter conflicts where one ethnic group is now seeking to obliterate another.

THE INTERNATIONAL COMMITTEE of the Red Cross has a mandate under international law to enforce and uphold the Geneva Conventions. This gives it rights not enjoyed by the other humanitarian organizations: the authority to visit and register all prisoners of war, to supervise exchanges, and to instruct combatants in the laws of war. The key question is whether this framework of law is suited to the chaotic conditions of the post–Cold War world. Are the new warriors still fighting by the old rules? The Gulf War, for instance, was fought by the Americans with the provisos of the conventions in mind. One of Norman

Schwarzkopf's staff officers has even claimed that Desert Storm was the most legal war America has ever fought. Lawyers versed in international law advised the army on targeting decisions, so that the war could be publicly perceived to be a clean one. The I.C.R.C. had doubts about some of those decisions—such as ones that left the children of Baghdad without water or sewage treatment—but the aftermath went strictly by the Geneva Conventions. Hundreds of thousands of prisoners of war were placed in camps in Saudi Arabia, and were then visited and released under I.C.R.C. auspices, as the conventions provide.

The problem for the Red Cross is that the Gulf War is one of the few recent hostilities in which parties have complied with the Geneva Conventions. Violations occur in *all* conflicts, even between combatants who are both signatories to the conventions. But Red Cross delegates are now encountering a kind of war that Dunant could never have imagined. Of the nearly fifty conflicts today, few conform to the classic pattern of professional war between states. They include army insurrections and guerrilla campaigns against unpopular regimes, ethnic-minority uprisings against majority rule, and jackal gangs roaming freely amid failed states. In these conflicts, civilians are always in the line of fire. In Algeria, Colombia, and Sri Lanka, civilians are targeted by irregular militias as often as any military objectives are. In Angola and Mozambique, the bush armies in conflict were so equally balanced that the wars ended only after the societies in which they were being fought had been destroyed; the same kind of war of attrition is occurring in southern Sudan today. In Afghanistan and Chechnya, wars that began as genuine national uprisings against foreign occupation have degenerated into vicious fights for territory, resources, drugs, and arms among militias who are often no different from criminal gangs. These wars are of little interest to great powers—there is no territorial or security interest at stake—and they can therefore be allowed to go on forever. In the decaying states of central and east Africa (Zaire, Rwanda, Burundi), in the Latin American states riven by drug wars and guerrilla insurgencies (Colombia, Peru), and along the inflamed border between the new Islamic and the old Soviet empires (Uzbekistan, Tajikistan, Turkmenistan, Azerbaijan), "ragged war," as the counterinsurgency specialist Leroy Thompson calls it, has become a relentless feature of daily life.

In the Solferino era, the purpose of war was to defeat the military forces of the other side. With Hitler, the purpose of war changed. It now includes terrorizing, deporting, and even exterminating the other side's civilian populations. For the Geneva Conventions to work, there have to be armies sufficiently disciplined to observe the distinction between combatants and civilians, between military and nonmilitary objectives. But what happens when there is no discipline at all? In Liberia, the civil war, which began in 1989 with a rebel-army insurrection against a corrupt government, has left more than a hundred and fifty thousand people dead and over a million people—about half the population—homeless as a result of factions fighting to control the drug and diamond trades. As many as six thousand of the combatants, according to some estimates, have been children. Child soldiers know nothing of Dunant's codes of honor. In Liberia, child soldiers held up I.C.R.C. convoys at checkpoints on the empty roads outside the capital, Monrovia. These children, in bomber jackets and running shoes, and with rocket-propelled grenade launchers on their shoulders or semiautomatic rifles on their hips, strutted about among the corpses. Wearing masks daubed with red paint, they had assumed noms de guerre like Major Rambo, Captain Double-Trouble, and General Snake. At the checkpoints, Red Cross workers reported, most of these masked figures were heavily drugged, and hadn't the slightest idea who or what they were fighting for. They robbed I.C.R.C. vehicles without compunction.

Graça Machel, the widow of the former president of Mozambique, has made a study of such child soldiers for the United Nations. There are many reasons why they are being recruited: the decay of indigenous warrior traditions that disdain the use of children in a man's vocation; the endemic character of many of these conflicts that create huge populations of orphans and displaced children who are easily recruited into the private armies, militias, and paramilitary bands. Graça Machel also observed that modern weapons technology makes it easy to use child soldiers: modern automatic weapons are so light and so easily taken apart and put together again that they can be put in the hands of children. In the mountains of northern Iraq, I have watched squads of young female Kurdish guerrillas firing rocket-propelled grenades from launchers taller than they were. In at least twenty-five of the current armed conflicts, there may be several hundred thousand child soldiers. In most traditional societies, honor is associated with restraint, and virility with discipline. In the manly bearing of many old Afghan warriors, or in the dignity of the Kurdish *peshmerga,* there is a martial order that is also a proud vision of male identity. The particular savagery of war in the 1990s taps into another vision of male identity—the wild sexuality of the adolescent male. Adolescents are supplying armies with a different kind of soldier—one for whom a weapon is not a thing to be respected or treated with ritual correctness but instead has an explicit phallic dimension. To traverse a checkpoint in Bosnia where adolescent boys in dark glasses and tight-fitting combat khakis wield AK-47s is to enter a zone of toxic testosterone. War has always had its sexual dimension—a soldier's uniform is no guarantee of good conduct—but when a war is conducted by adolescent irregulars, sexual savagery becomes one of its regular weapons.

THROUGHOUT THE TWENTIETH CENTURY, humanitarian law has been running an uneven race with the demonic inventiveness of military technology and the protean and ever-changing face of modern war. When the Geneva Conventions were revised in 1949, Article 3 extended their scope to civil wars and other non-international conflicts. Article 13 recognized that, in these new types of insurgencies, combatants wouldn't necessarily wear soldiers' uniforms. In the new world of war, the mark of a warrior was no longer his uniform; it was his weapon. Anyone "carrying arms openly," it decreed, was entitled to the conventions' protection. Then, in 1977, two protocols were added, one of which authorized the International Committee of the Red Cross to intervene in wars of national liberation and in internal campaigns of civil disobedience, like the Palestinian uprising. The United States, Britain, and Israel, among others, have not yet ratified these additional protocols, believing that the I.C.R.C.'s presence in such internal wars legitimizes insurgents at the expense of sovereign states. But even when the I.C.R.C. is allowed access to insurgent groups, it faces a more serious problem: finding someone in charge. The conventions speak of dissident armies' being under "responsible command." In the 1990s, most of the fighting is done by irregulars—the casualties of collapsing societies—or by paramilitary gangs that combine banditry with soldiery. As war passes out of the hands of the state into those of warlords, the rituals of restraint associated with the profession of arms also disintegrate. The I.C.R.C.'s work has become more dangerous. In Rwanda alone in 1994, the Red Cross movement lost thirty-six workers to acts of war, in part because it was specifically targeted for attack. And 1996 was one of the worst years in the I.C.R.C.'s long history. In Burundi, in June, a Land Cruiser containing three delegates was ambushed and shot at; the vehicle plunged into a ravine, killing all inside. In Chechnya, in December 1996, six Red Cross field staff were murdered in their beds in a hospital outside Grozny. Almost every delegate I have talked to has lived through a moment of pure terror. For Pascal Mauchle, a member of the Afghanistan delegation, it was crossing a front line into a no-man's-land in an unarmed white Land Cruiser, unsure whether the road ahead was free from mines, or whether the gunmen at the last checkpoint could be believed when they said it was safe, or whether the gunmen at the next checkpoint would shoot when they saw his vehicle coming into view.

The new fears for the security of I.C.R.C. delegates involve the organization in dilemmas that go to the very heart of its neutrality. If Red Cross delegates were dispatched in United Nations convoys, they would have the protection of U.N. armor, but the organization's reputation for independence would be compromised. Even providing delegates with flak jackets and Kevlar helmets and bulletproofing their Land Cruisers have occasioned heated debate. If you harden the target, so the argument has gone, you only increase the likelihood of its becoming a target. If you trust the militias, they will trust you. But delegates have paid for this trust with their lives. In a recent paper, an Oxford professor of international relations, Adam Roberts, was scathing about the I.C.R.C.'s reliance on the prestige of its reputation: "Constructive thinking about security is . . . not assisted by the tradition, in itself honourable, of associating humanitarian action with impartiality and neutrality: sometimes the provision of security may necessitate departures from these principles."

Without departing from its principles, the Red Cross *has* begun to change its security procedures. It now posts armed guards to protect the homes of its delegates; there are armed guards, too, around its medical depots and food warehouses to prevent looting. As far as hospitals, clinics, and medical centers and the interior of its own delegations are concerned, weapons are banned. But perimeter security is provided, and it is armed.

I I

IT WAS YUGOSLAVIA that first showed the Red Cross the new face of modern war. In June 1991, war broke out between Serbia and Croatia. On November 18, five months into the conflict, the I.C.R.C. delegate Nicolas Borsinger got word that the fall of Vukovar, a Croatian town of forty thousand people on the banks of the Danube, was fast approaching. Borsinger had been waiting near the Hungarian border while for three months Vukovar was shelled by the Serb-dominated Yugoslav National Army. The town had become the Croatian Stalingrad. Borsinger bluffed his way through the Serbian lines by claiming that he had an appointment with "the General." The town was a scene of devastation: hardly a building was standing. Drunken Serbs were carousing in the streets and firing into the air while others were pulling Croatian civilians out of their bunkers and basements and rounding them up. "Everything pointed to an imminent massacre," Borsinger recalled. He gained access to the municipal hospital, which was under the supervision of a Serbian captain and was overcrowded with injured Croatian civilians. After several hours, the captain grew impatient with Borsinger, and Borsinger decided he had better leave. That same day, the I.C.R.C. worked out an agreement to neutralize the hospital and put it under its own supervision. But radio communications were down, and word of the agreement never reached Vukovar. When Borsinger returned the next day, he was detained at a checkpoint, where he saw three trucks being driven away by Serb militiamen. In them were two hundred and ten people, patients and hospital staff; they were never seen again. A mass grave was discovered at Ovcara, a nearby village, a year later. When the grave was exhumed, some of the victims were wearing hospital gowns and had I.V.s still attached to their arms.

The atrocities in Vukovar—and many of the worst war crimes committed elsewhere in the former Yugoslavia—were carried out by paramilitary bands under the command of Serbian warlords and criminal operators with connections in politics, business, and the Belgrade underworld. "White Eagles" was one such group, led by Duke Seselj, a protofascist politician in Belgrade. "Tigers," led by "Arkan," was the name of another. Arkan was a Belgrade mobster, wanted in Sweden on an international warrant for murder. He had parlayed his fame as a paramilitary into a mobster's empire that ranged from Belgrade ice-cream parlors to gas stations.

During my own journey through the former Yugoslavia in 1993, I came across the signs of Arkan's presence. In one Serbian farmhouse in a zone conquered from the Croats in 1991, I saw an Arkan calendar hanging on the wall, like a protecting icon in the corner of the farmhouse kitchen. Arkan was posing with a paramilitary squad in combat fatigues holding up a fancy Uzi machine pistol. These were the irregular private armies, trained and licensed by the Serbian regime in Belgrade—though the Croatians had HOS, a paramilitary equivalent of their own—who did the dirty work neither regime allowed its regular armies to do. Arkan and Seselj's men had "cleansed" the Croatian villages of eastern Slavonia in 1991; in 1992, they had swept down the east side of the Drina, killing and torturing Muslims, driving them out of their homelands on the border with Serbia.

On that same journey in 1993, I visited the ruins of Vukovar. Seselj's White Eagles had set up headquarters in the only large building left standing in Vukovar after the Serbs had taken it from the Croatian defenders eighteen months earlier. The men, wearing combat fatigues and black toques, stood guard in the windswept expanse of what had once been a civic square and asked me why I was nosing around the ruins, in the company of a local journalist. They were large, long-haired, snub-nosed men— part warrior, part thug. I said the local journalist was my friend and was helping with translation. They said he was from the local Hungarian minority, and if they caught him telling lies about Serbia, they would kill him. I said I didn't like to be threatened. They said I had been warned. Later that night, warning shots were fired at our car from somewhere in the darkened ruins. We left Vukovar the next morning.

Irregulars are as old as war itself, and their savagery is proverbial. But in times past, armies managed to co-opt irregular militias, introduce regimental discipline, and bring their violence under state control. The Cossacks were domesticated by the armies of the czar; the Highland clans were beaten back and then absorbed into the Highland Regiments. The irregulars of the Balkan wars are historically distinctive, in that instead of being co-opted and tamed by the state, they were covertly instigated by states—Serbia and Croatia—to perform atrocities, not as an unintended consequence of drunkenness and indiscipline, but as a deliberate military strategy. Men were recruited from prisons, trained in secret army camps, and equipped with the best weaponry from state armories. The irregulars were created to provide the state with officially deniable ethnic cleansing. A war was franchised to private enterprise, in order to dispense with any of the moral accountability associated with professional soldiery.

In May 1992—six months after the fall of Vukovar—the war entered Bosnia. The I.C.R.C. dispatched a convoy of medical supplies to Sarajevo, the Bosnian capital, under the command of one of its most charismatic delegates, Frederic Maurice. His convoy set out from Belgrade, stopped at the Serb capital of Pale, and then proceeded to Sarajevo. Inside the city, the convoy—five vehicles, all painted white, with the Red Cross logo unmistakable—passed the Serb checkpoint without incident. Before it reached the Muslim checkpoint, it came under fire from unknown gunmen. The Red Cross still won't officially say who was responsible. For forty-five minutes, the convoy was stranded while rockets and small-arms fire rained down upon it. Eventually, Muslim militiamen appeared and pointed the way to safety. Maurice was pulled out of a bullet-riddled Land Cruiser and taken to a hospital; he died after undergoing emergency surgery. Bosnia is about two hours' flying time from Switzerland. Alpine meadows and mountain streams remind Swiss delegates of home. Bosnia's leaders repeatedly promised to observe the Geneva Conventions; its armies were trained in the European laws of war. Within two years, however, they had invented a type of war that allowed states to deny their responsibilities under the Geneva Conventions. They had also invented a type of fighter who did not scruple to target a Red Cross convoy. From Geneva, the I.C.R.C. ordered its delegates to pull out of Bosnia and Herzegovina in late May, and none returned for five weeks.

Those five weeks turned out to be the worst of the war: Muslim towns and mosques were blown up, and burial grounds were dug up. Among the first I.C.R.C. delegates to return was Patrick Gasser, and in Manjaca, near Banja Luka, in northern Bosnia, he came upon a sight that taxed his powers of description. In hot corrugated-metal sheds built for livestock, Gasser found about twenty-three hundred Muslim detainees—noncombatant civilian males, gaunt, hollow-eyed, and in a state of shock. The men were so emaciated that the I.C.R.C. brought in a nutritionist from the Somalia famine to oversee a feeding program. Gasser flew back to Geneva to report on what he had seen. At first, he could not get his superiors to understand that concentration camps had returned to Europe. For two weeks, I.C.R.C. executives sat on Gasser's information and debated what to do. If they spoke out publicly, they might jeopardize the I.C.R.C.'s capacity to help the victims. If they kept silent, they became accomplices to ethnic cleansing, and just possibly to genocide.

ALMOST EXACTLY FIFTY YEARS BEFORE, the Red Cross had faced a similar dilemma. On October 14, 1942, the committee of twenty-three Swiss politicians, lawyers, doctors, and businessmen who ran the international Red Cross met to consider the evidence from their delegates about the deportation of civilian populations in occupied Europe. In strictly legal terms, civilians were none of the Red Cross's business: the Geneva Conventions as they stood in 1939 granted Red Cross delegates the right only to visit prisoners of war. But in the course of these visits, Red Cross delegates had heard rumors of deportations; had watched sealed trains leaving for destinations in the east; had driven past concentration camps. When they had made inquiries about these camps to the head of the German Red Cross, Ernst Grawitz, he told them that this matter was none of Geneva's business. Grawitz knew whose business it was: he was not only head of the Red Cross but also chief medical officer of the SS, one of the men responsible for the secret medical experimentation on camp inmates.

Though the gates of the concentration camps were shut to the Red Cross, Geneva had some inkling of what was going on inside. In the course of a visit to Berlin, Carl Burckhardt, a senior member of the Red Cross executive committee, had been told by a senior German official that Hitler had signed an order in early 1941 decreeing that by the end of 1942 "there would no longer be any Jews in Germany." When Burckhardt reported this to the American consul in Geneva, the consul asked him whether this meant extermination. Burckhardt replied that it couldn't mean anything else.

By late September the I.C.R.C. had drafted a public appeal that, while not mentioning Jews or any other group by name, condemned the deportations and forced labor inflicted on civilian populations. When the project came to a vote, Carl Burckhardt opposed the public appeal altogether. Lofty public appeals to international morality were not likely to have the slightest impact on Hitler, he argued, and they would only jeopardize the Red Cross's existing access to prisoners of war. The representative of the Swiss government, terrified that a public declaration might even jeopardize Swiss neutrality, also counseled caution. "Isn't it the case that the good Samaritan never breaks his silence except by his deeds?" The public appeal was never issued. The Red Cross kept silent about what it knew throughout the war.

When the Germans occupied Hungary in 1944, the I.C.R.C. delegate Friedrich Born managed to protect some Jewish orphanages and hospitals by placing them under Red Cross supervision and by giving Red Cross documents to thousands of Jews who worked in these institutions. But he was unable to secure exit visas for any of them, and in late 1944 he had to watch helplessly while fifty thousand Budapest Jews were rounded up and marched on foot to their destruction in Germany.

Delegates in Germany and Poland were completely barred from the camps. Delegates passing Mauthausen in 1944 saw smoke issuing from the crematoria. Other delegates visiting Allied prisoners of war in a camp in Poland heard about showers in a place called Auschwitz where civilians were gassed. But they had no opportunity to verify these rumors. They never saw the reality inside until the Reich collapsed in the spring of 1945. By then Ernst Grawitz, SS doctor and head of the German Red Cross, had committed suicide—just before the full nature of his experiments on inmates became known.

In 1992, in contrast to 1942, silence proved impossible: the world press had found its own way to the camps near Banja Luka. Roy Gutman, of *Newsday*, was there. The I.C.R.C. had always treated journalists with suspicion, but in this instance it collaborated with them. Without divulging details of the I.C.R.C.'s findings, Gasser provided the corroboration necessary for *Newsday* to run its first stories. A week later, the British news organization ITN cornered the Bosnian Serb leader Radovan Karadzic in London and extracted a promise from him to let ITN send a TV crew to film in the camps. The Red Cross delegates on the scene watched the ensuing media circus with disbelief. The realities on the ground, which were complicated enough, were immediately repackaged in the moral narrative of the Holocaust. The camps that the media actually got to see were not death camps but transit camps for civilian detainees whom the Serbs hoped to send into exile. Indeed, the barbed wire was being removed from Trnopole as the film crews arrived. Nonetheless, the film clip that ITN shot of emaciated Muslim men standing mutely behind barbed wire became the most resonant image of the entire Bosnian war. For the Red Cross delegates on the scene, the moral equation between ethnic cleansing and the Holocaust was highly dubious. It soon became evident to them that the Serbs, in inviting the world's press, were cynically exploiting the West's Holocaust memories and inveigling Western governments into taking in Muslim refugees and thus abetting the ethnic cleansing of central Bosnia. The Serbs even managed to enlist the I.C.R.C. in that project: by Christmas of 1992, the I.C.R.C. had overseen the closing of all the camps in northern Bosnia and transferred most of their inmates to transit camps in Croatia and elsewhere in Europe.

Throughout the Bosnian war, the I.C.R.C. struggled to devise a way to protect civilians without being the unwilling agent of ethnic cleansing. In October 1992, Cornelio Sommaruga proposed that certain Muslim towns be declared safe havens. In April 1993, with these towns on the brink of capture by the Serbs, the United Nations Security Council adopted Sommaruga's idea, which by then had considerable backing. Safe havens were a traditional concept in the European laws of war—Dunant had proposed such an idea to protect Paris in 1870—but Sommaruga's idea could only have worked if three conditions had been met: The Muslims did not use the havens as military bases, and the Serbs respected their neutrality. Neither side kept its part of the bargain. The third condition was that U.N. member states would commit thirty-five thousand soldiers to the defense of the enclaves. In the event, only seven thousand were sent. Srebrenica was guarded by not more than several hundred. Moral promises were made to innocent civilians that anyone close to the situation, including the Red Cross, knew could not be kept.

In July 1995, Serbian militiamen fought their way into the haven, disarmed the United Nations peacekeepers there, rounded up all the men in town, and evicted the women and children, as well as the local Red Cross staff. The I.C.R.C. had only local Bosnian staff in the town—its delegates were based in nearby Tuzla. Now these delegates watched helplessly as some twenty-three thousand women and children staggered across battle lines and through minefields to the Tuzla air base. There a vast international relief effort was set up to care for them; thanks to the news cameras on the scene, as many as fifty humanitarian agencies were soon clamoring to help the women and children as they arrived. The Red Cross, crowded out in the humanitarian scramble, decided to focus on tracing the victims. Its delegates set up a tent at the air base, and for a week the women of Srebrenica trooped through it, telling stories of how their men had been led away at gunpoint by the Serbian militiamen. Even then, it was plain to everyone that most of those who had disappeared—and the I.C.R.C. counted about seven thousand in all—had already been executed. A handful of young female delegates had to absorb the full force of the Srebrenica women's grief and fury. The emotional stress was so great that one delegate had to be evacuated to Geneva.

The widows of Srebrenica are housed in dormitories on the outskirts of Tuzla, converted gymnasiums, schools, ex-convents, and former restaurants. The bunks are crowded tight against each other, forty to a room; hanging from the bedsteads are the women's possessions stored in plastic bags. The women are country people, most of them, in kerchiefs and baggy trousers, and they shuffle from their bunks to the bathrooms and dining rooms in their old carpet slippers. Their tread is listless; they sit by the hour and stare out of the window. They are waiting. For justice. For an answer. For time to resume its course. And now they know, most of them, that their men will never return. When they tell you their stories, they beat their fists against their knees and they weep.

They want justice, but the I.C.R.C. and other humanitarian organizations who look after them are not in the business of justice. It is the War Crimes Tribunal at the Hague that must give them justice. Yet, despite having the largest and most reliable databases on the victims of massacre, despite having helped journalists reveal the story of the Bosnian camps, the I.C.R.C. has refused to share its information with the tribunal. Its doctrine of neutrality and confidentiality prevents it from doing so. Delegates like Beat Schweitzer and Patrick Gasser argue heatedly that they would never have gained access to Trnopole and Manjaca if the Serb authorities had known that the Red Cross would turn over information to war crimes tribunals. They believe that they cannot be seen to assist in bringing war criminals to justice if they wish to have access to the prisoners and victims held by these war criminals. This policy, as morally ambiguous as it may seem, has also had an unexpected dividend. In 1995, when NATO F-16s were prowling over Banja Luka picking apart Serbian air defenses during the joint Croat-Muslim offensive, the Red Cross was the only humanitarian organization allowed to remain in Serb-held Bosnia and Croatia. All other organizations, associated as they were with NATO-member states, had to leave. This meant that when the Croat-Muslim offensive in Bosnia and the Croatian attack on the Krajina Serbs began to create huge numbers of Serbian refugees, the Red Cross was there to help them. It is one of the ironies of the war that the largest single act of ethnic cleansing in the conflict—the Croatian clearance of Krajina, which drove six hundred thousand Serbs back into Serbia—was committed against the population whom the world held responsible for introducing the term into the language. The I.C.R.C. was able to feed and clothe the refugees. Neutrality, in relation to the War Crimes Tribunal, may have been controversial, but it allowed the

Red Cross to be there when perpetrator was suddenly transformed into victim.

The I.C.R.C.'s experience in Yugoslavia shook the organization to the core. Its delegates had shown extraordinary devotion and courage, but many of them were oppressed with a sense of failure and futility. The I.C.R.C. arrived in Vukovar hours too late, and hundreds were killed; it was dispatched to Sarajevo only to be attacked; it discovered concentration camps and then became an inadvertent accomplice to ethnic cleansing; and it joined in the international clamor for safe havens only to watch helplessly as the havens became a trap, and finally a tomb, for seven thousand men. It was one thing to see the Geneva Conventions ignored in a non-European city, but to see how little their principles meant a few hours from Geneva was genuinely shocking. Many delegates openly wondered whether the International Committee of the Red Cross had lost its way, or else asked if the world had changed so much that the organization no longer had a place in it.

III

THE INTERNATIONAL COMMITTEE of the Red Cross is proud of its program in Afghanistan, and it has reason to be: It feeds a large number of people, has rebuilt the shattered limbs of mine victims, visits prisoners on all sides of the conflict, and has taught the mujahideen, versed in the pitiless logic of jihad, the laws of war. But how do you judge a program a success in a country where a million people have died since 1979?

In late September 1996, the I.C.R.C. invited me to visit its field operation there. A week before I was due to arrive, I got a call from Geneva telling me that Taliban militias had broken through the government lines southeast of Kabul, that the United Nations and some aid agencies were evacuating nonessential personnel from the city, and that the I.C.R.C., as usual, would in large part remain. Did I still want to go?

By the time I arrived in Peshawar, Kabul had fallen. I hitched a ride on the second relief flight into the city. The airport is ringed by rounded hills, burned bare of all vegetation. The dusty scrim at the edge of the runways is littered with wingless MiGs and gutted Tupolevs, the detritus left behind by the Russians' final departure in 1992. The airport itself, which had been built by the Soviets, was now scarcely functioning: its windows were blown out, its baggage hall was darkened, and the conveyor belts were still and covered in dust. Squatting at the edge of the runway was a cluster of Taliban fighters—turbaned, baggy-trousered, leaning on Kalashnikovs. Behind them was a Mitsubishi Pajero with rocket-propelled grenade launchers.

Talib means "religious student," and the movement began in the Islamic seminaries in Pakistan in the early 1990s. By 1994, the Taliban militias, armed and trained by the Pakistanis, had begun their march to claim Afghanistan while enforcing the strictest version of Islamic law ever encountered in the Muslim world: prohibiting women from employment; forcing them to wear the *burka*, with its hateful lattice grille over the face; stoning adulterers; and amputating the hands of thieves. Now the Taliban controlled the capital and three-quarters of the country.

In my journeys I have seen a certain amount of desolation: the ruins of Vukovar, the pitted and pocked concrete ghost town that is Huambo in Angola. But in the landscape of endemic war, Kabul is in a class of desolation all its own. It is the Dresden of post–Cold War conflict: mile upon mile of rubble and dust, abandoned and windswept, populated here and there by ragged families eking out their survival inside abandoned truck containers that have been sawed in half. Ranging up the hillsides were thousands of roofless and windowless houses, deserted by their former inhabitants. The warring militias had spared nothing: the blue-domed mosques, the minarets, the hospitals, the schools. The Kabul museum, which once housed a collection of early Buddhist relics, lay open to the sky, its ancient columns lying about on the roadside, its collection looted. The Soviet Embassy and the Soviet cultural center had been ripped apart, and Taliban artillery detachments were scuttling about in the ruins.

In 1992, when the Soviet-backed regime of Muhammad Najibullah crumbled after an army mutiny, he and his brother had sought refuge in a U.N. guesthouse in Kabul, and Najibullah stayed there for four years. Three nights before I arrived, the Taliban had dragged him out of the guesthouse, castrated him, and beaten him to death, and then hanged his pulpy body from the stanchion of a traffic warden's observation tower. As I drove into the city, only the noose, flecked with blood, remained swinging from the tower.

The I.C.R.C. headquarters, in the center of Kabul, was hidden behind piles of sandbags. Its lintels were reinforced with rough-hewn timber supports. A dozen white Land Cruisers were parked in the yard, each with a COMITÉ INTERNATIONALE GENÈVE decal on its doors and the sign of a Kalashnikov with two red slashes through it: no weapons allowed in I.C.R.C. cars, no weapons in the compound. Unarmed local employees frisked everyone who came through the gates.

In the days since the Taliban takeover, I learned, the I.C.R.C. had been opening up lines of communication to the rebel commanders who were running the city. "Running the city" is a euphemism. Actually, Kabul was without a government. The Taliban leaders had commandeered every available vehicle and rushed north to chase government forces farther into the mountains. The detachments left behind to administer the city were not doing a lot of administering. Many of the prisons had been emptied, and the Red Cross compound was filling up with former prisoners bearing yellow I.C.R.C. registration cards and seeking relief. The hallways, especially those adjacent to the satellite phone, were crowded with journalists, avid to cover the Taliban takeover, though Kabul, from their point of view, was distressingly free of televisable signs of recent carnage. Struggling to cope with them was an I.C.R.C. press delegate, a former journalist with South African radio who was now enlisted in the "cause," as he called it, half ironically. Press delegates are a recent addition to the I.C.R.C.'s field presence in the war zones. It is no longer enough to be there. The I.C.R.C. must be *seen* to be there: otherwise donor nations may begin to ask why their generosity remains invisible.

The Afghanistan delegation head was Michel Ducraux. His office had reproductions of Vermeers and Matisses, shatterproof plastic windows, and a view entirely blocked by sandbags piled eight feet high. Ducraux is a lean, elegant man in his early fifties. He appeared coolly reflective and seemed to keep cynicism and commitment in a subtle inner equilibrium. His view of the war embraced its paradoxes. The entire delegation, he recalled, had recently spent the day in shelters below the compound as Muslim militias rocketed the city, huddled for hours in a dark, cramped shelter while providing medical assistance to militias bent on destroying each other, and preaching restraint to Islamic warriors who among them have reduced their own city to rubble. It was *"hyper-désagréable,"* Ducraux said.

The Afghans are border people, on the spiny buffer between civilizations—Iran, India, Central Asia—and have fought everyone from Alexander to the British army to keep a stubborn independence alive. They have a reputation as being among the most redoubtable guerrillas of all time. Their tradition of fighting—based on small, mobile units that avoid direct attack or pitched battle, seeking instead to use the mountain passes to ambush the enemy and surround it—was what brought them victory against the Russians. It was a tradition that respected the ecology of a poor society and the climate of a mountainous one: war began once the crop was planted or the animals were put up in the pastures, and it stopped when the harvest came and the snows descended. War was endemic, but it was self-limiting.

Once the warlords had ceased to be united against an external enemy, however, they began turning against each other. The radicalization of Islam made things worse: instead of bringing the militias together, religious principle now set them at gunpoint. And the weapons left behind by the Russians, and those shipped in by the Americans—from tanks to Stinger missiles—were so powerful that they overwhelmed the self-limiting ecology of warrior traditions. Afghan warriors of the past did not target mosques and minarets, hospitals and schools. Kabul is the graveyard of the Afghan warriors' honor.

So what was the I.C.R.C. doing here now? Ducraux was characteristically philosophical. "What is more human than war?" he mused. The organization was not here to stop war, and even its attempts to humanize it had proved futile. "We're here to reduce the damage," he said. "To feed the widows, to visit the prisoners, to fit new limbs on the bodies of those torn apart by mines." War was absurd but inevitable. What else was there, the International Committee of the Red Cross seemed to be saying, but the modest morality of small deeds?

IT WAS NOT EASY to meet the Taliban fighters. Most were in the Pansheer Valley, to the northeast of Kabul, and those left behind to guard the city were hostile to foreigners. But there was a detachment in residence at the Intercontinental Hotel, an improbable wedge of sixties brutalism miraculously still perched on top of one of Kabul's hills, with a panoramic view of the devastation. Tanks and artillery were deployed in the pine groves around the hotel car park. With an I.C.R.C. interpreter—he had prudently doffed his Western jacket and donned a small white cap (his stubble had been growing for several days)—I approached a detachment of Taliban sitting on the grass by the drained hotel pool and looking out over the dusty haze of Kabul. They were sitting cross-legged, their bearded faces framed by their turbans, and were languidly dismembering roses from the hotel gardens or turning over worry beads in their fingers. They had new watches and new shoes.

I asked what they were fighting for, and they turned to the one who was apparently the most educated of them—a fierce young seminarian with a Western haircut and a long beard. "For Islam," he said. "To stop the fighting among the brothers. And to have an Islamic state."

But then, I asked, why are the brothers still killing one another?

"The Prophet Muhammad, may his name be blessed, instructed us that when corruption is on the earth one must fight to bring peace."

The next morning, the Taliban identified an example of corruption—in the very cellars of the Intercontinental. Fourteen hundred cans of beer and eighteen hundred bottles of "alcoholic drinks" were dragged out and piled up in the car park. After prayers and a short speech by the head of the Taliban religious police (a force whose name means "the Department of Command of Good and Injunction of the Unlawful"), the bottles were ceremonially smashed and the cans crushed, while an invited audience of parched Western journalists looked on in undisguised dismay.

When I returned from the Intercontinental to the I.C.R.C. compound, I found that furniture was being moved into the courtyard. Turbaned Afghans were struggling past, carrying chairs and tables. Two women delegates—an office administrator and a nurse—had put on head scarves and Afghan trousers. The Afghan women—who run the message system, maintain files on prisoner-of-war visits, and trace prisoners and missing persons—were being moved out of sight into a separate block, behind a wall of sandbags. The Red Cross was reorganizing its offices to keep the women hidden and the Taliban happy.

Thomas Gurtner, the deputy head of the I.C.R.C. in Kabul, had just returned from a meeting with other relief agencies— Oxfam, Médecins sans Frontières, UNICEF, and the United Nations High Commission on Refugees. All ran programs that employed Afghan women. All were protesting against the Taliban decrees that suspended women from their jobs, forcing them to return to their homes and to the dominion of their husbands and fathers. These agencies had been calling upon the I.C.R.C. to join their appeal. Gurtner had refused.

I asked him whether he considered women's rights a humanitarian issue.

"Of course not," he replied briskly.

I was beginning to understand that the laws of war are one thing and human rights quite another. The I.C.R.C. enforces the laws of war; it is not a human rights organization. It does not campaign against injustice. Its legitimacy depends on its working with warriors and warlords: if they insist that women be kept out of sight, it has no choice but to go along.

TO ACCEPT the Taliban position on women is, to say the least, to be a moral relativist. How then does the I.C.R.C. reconcile this relativism with its defense of the Geneva Conventions, which are a universalist and universalizing code? How do you teach the warrior's code of honor to men trained in Islamic jihad? How do you teach the laws of war to people who may never have heard of the Geneva Conventions?

The I.C.R.C. delegate in charge of "dissemination" in Kabul was Jean-Pascal Moret. At forty-two, Jampa— his radio call sign— -is older than most Red Cross field-workers. He has no university degree, sometimes drives a taxi in Geneva between his Red Cross missions, and is a practicing Tibetan Buddhist.

As Jampa observed, everything that the Red Cross does is dissemination· If you drive your Land Cruiser too fast in the streets of Kabul, you give the whole delegation a reputation for arrogance; if you talk back to a Taliban at a checkpoint, the next Land Cruiser that goes through may get fired upon. Dissemination, in other words, means preserving the moral currency of the Red Cross symbol. If the Afghan program is a "success," that is largely because the symbol still retains legitimacy among all the factions. The I.C.R.C. can't stop the flow of arms from Pakistan and Russia; it can't force a cease-fire or a truce. It can only try to get the factions to observe some basic rules: Don't shoot the wounded; don't fire on ambulances; don't target hospitals; don't attack civilians; don't torture prisoners. It is gambling on the proposition that however different warrior cultures may be, across the world, they can at least agree on this basic minimum. Even so, this basic minimum, however universal it may seem, has to be translated into local moral vernaculars.

A generation ago, the I.C.R.C. made few concessions to local culture. Before I set out for Kabul, one veteran, Pierre

Gassmann—who is now the head of the I.C.R.C. delegation in Colombia—told me that dissemination had changed radically since he joined the organization, in the late sixties. "First, we threw our book at them," he said. "Then we threw theirs. Now we don't know what book to throw at them. We're trying something a little more subtle."

In Somalia, the Red Cross runs theater groups that perform both for the various clans and for groups of gunmen; the delegation has hired singers and poets to record songs about—believe it or not—the laws of war, and the songs and dramas are played on the BBC World Service. In Chechnya, first-aid teams distribute a shoulder bandage printed with cartoons showing warriors lifting the wounded from the battlefield, escorting orphans to safety, and rounding up prisoners and taking them into custody. But the biggest challenge is how to teach the European rules of war to radical Islam.

In medieval Europe, there was a distinction between *bellum hostile* (warfare characterized by restraint) and *bellum romanum* (warfare, in the words of the historian Michael Howard, "in which no holds were barred and all those designated as enemy, whether bearing arms or not, would be indiscriminately slaughtered"). Medieval Christendom carried this distinction into the Crusades against Islam: unmitigated ferocity reserved for unbelievers. Islam responded in kind; jihad was its very own *bellum romanum*. The moral particularism of these traditions, which distinguish between worthy and unworthy victims, stands in contrast to the moral universalism of the Geneva Conventions, which call on soldiers to respect all victims.

If Europe's own warrior traditions were always highly particularist, how did the ambition to universalize them, and to make them genuinely universal, come into being? One of the central emotions of the European Enlightenment—especially evident, for example, in Voltaire's scathing diatribes against the Spanish Inquisition and the cruelties of the wars of religion—was a loathing at the way religious ethics were used to justify persecution and slaughter. It was a loathing at the way in which the self-styled universalism of Christian ethics masked and justified an exterminatory particularism, directed against heretics, savages, and unbelievers. Out of this Enlightenment rage at Christian hypocrisy came a concerted attempt to frame a universalist ethics based on supposed facts of human nature, especially our universal susceptibility to pain and cruelty. It cannot be accidental that this concern to rescue ethics from religious particularism and ground it in human nature occurred as European voyages of discovery and the opening-up of empire revealed the staggering diversity of culture, ethics, and belief around the world. The Red Cross is the heir of this Enlightenment revolt against religious particularism, the bearer of the Enlightenment faith that while cultures may differ in what they respect and value, all cultures give approximately the same meaning to pain and suffering. Beneath the particular, the universal; beneath difference, identity: this is the modern faith on which humanitarian action depends.

In searching for universals to appeal to in Islamic culture, the I.C.R.C. has looked beyond the jihad tradition. Four years ago, for instance, the organization had printed in Cairo an illustrated paperback, *Chronicles of Islamic-Arab History,* with the key provisions of the Geneva Conventions matched with bits of traditional Arab and Islamic wisdom. The book inscribes the counsels of a Muslim warrior caliph, Ali ibn Abi Talib, who was a nephew of Muhammad:

> If you are victorious over them, do not stab them in the
> back! Do not kill the wounded or uncover their genitals!
> Do not mutilate the dead! Do not tear a veil!

Elsewhere there are the familiar injunctions of an ancient agricultural economy:

> Abstain from treachery; abstain from transgressing limits; abstain from betrayal; abstain from killing small children, old men, or women; abstain from cutting palm trees; abstain from slaughtering sheep or cows or camels except to feed yourselves.

In the Arab countries, Red Cross delegates retell the story of the Arab warrior sultan Saladin and his noble treatment of his prisoner Richard the Lionheart, the Crusader king. "Thus," the I.C.R.C. argues hopefully, "Islamic law has preceded the international community by more than a thousand years."

There is something attractive here—a determination to prove that the Red Cross's principles are not merely products of Swiss Calvinism but human universals, which can be found in all cultures. Equally, there is something poignant in the Red Cross's curious faith that human violence can be contained by injunctions from holy books. The Kabul office has printed similar injunctions in its calendars. These calendars, with their humanist messages, have been hanging in buildings surrounded by devastation.

Afghanistan, however, poses an additional problem. War is always at its most unrestrained when religion vests it with holy purpose, and the Taliban is perhaps the most militantly religious militia on earth. At checkpoints around the city, its fighters were searching cars for magazines and cassettes. I saw videotapes and audiotapes festooning a tree near one such checkpoint, and assumed they were pornographic, or rock and roll, or some kind of anti-Taliban propaganda. But I learned that the objective of the fighters is in fact much wider. They are searching for anything that depicts the human face or any of God's creatures. In no other Islamic society have the new revolutionary authorities gone so far. The imams of Iran have derided the Taliban's rigid belief in the pernicious effect of visual representations. As a result, the I.C.R.C.'s calendar, with its images of war amputees hobbling about in the gardens of the blue mosque at Hazar el Sharif and its benign messages from Islamic texts, will be kept out of sight. So will the comic book that the I.C.R.C. has distributed locally, in conjunction with a BBC radio drama on the life and hard times of Ali Gul, a fictitious Afghan hero. If the Taliban leaders have their way, all this patient and rather subtle work of translating the European laws of war into the vernacular of local warrior culture will be pulped. The eyes are the windows of the soul. And, according to the Taliban's very strict interpretation of the Koran, all depictions of the eye—all photographs, paintings, prints, videos, and films—are forbidden. Only God himself, the Taliban leaders say, should see into the windows of the soul.

AT THE HEART of the Geneva Conventions is the I.C.R.C.'s detention work, as it is called: the protection of military prisoners of war. The delegate in charge of visiting the Kabul prisoners is Pascal Mauchle, another one of the new breed that seems to welcome outside scrutiny by journalists, perhaps the better to co-opt them. He invited me to join him on a detention visit.

He had divided his team into three groups: two of them went to a prison recently discovered to be holding militiamen from the government side who had been taken by the Taliban during the capture of Kabul; the third went out into the city to investigate stories of summary arrests supposedly carried out by the Taliban security forces. I was assigned to one of the prison details.

The prison was a decrepit yellow structure with a straw roof and heavy stone walls. Taliban guards, backed up by a few Pakistani secret-service police, were lounging at the entrance to the long, dark cell blocks. The low cell doors were flimsy constructions made of wood, and the locks were perfunctory. We ducked low and entered a cell, approximately six feet by ten feet, that held eighteen prisoners squatting on dirty mattresses. A few plastic bags of belongings hung from nails on the walls. The smell of the cell was animal-close but clean. Through broken panes in a window you could hear car horns and hawkers' cries coming from Chicken Street.

The prisoners, who crowded around us, were disturbingly young: few, I soon learned, were older than eighteen, and several were not more than fourteen. Some barely had their first growth of beard. As an I.C.R.C. delegate, sitting cross-legged on the floor, began registering them, filling out a card of personal details for each prisoner, their stories came out in bits and pieces. They were mostly ethnic Tajiks. None of them admitted to being regular soldiers. They all claimed to have been working as peddlers, waiters, or garage mechanics, and to have been sucked into the militias because, in a collapsing economy, the militia on the government side offered them security, money, and food. But they hadn't proved to be very determined fighters. Having been posted to the southeastern outskirts of the city to repel the Taliban advance, they had surrendered—so they said—without firing a shot.

As the delegate took down one prisoner's details, I folded the yellow registration card of the preceding prisoner, slid it into a plastic folder, and handed it to him. Many received their cards with a little bow or with the Afghan gesture of placing a hand briefly over the heart. Then each slipped his card into the inside pocket of his brown waistcoat. There was something sacramental about this ritual. In jails, lockups, cages, and camps around the world, prisoners like these have been getting cards like these, their guarantee of such protection and moral concern as the Geneva Conventions can offer them. It is proof that they have not been forgotten, that some foreigner will make it his business to demand information if they go missing or show up at his next visit with bruises on their bodies.

But the yellow cards do not seem to be nearly enough. Once everyone was registered and had his card, the prisoners seemed to press forward. One spoke urgently to the delegate for a long time. When they were taken by the Taliban, they were promised amnesty. They wanted the Red Cross delegate to take up their cause.

The delegate gathered his papers. He was peremptory: Amnesty was none of his affair. The I.C.R.C. wasn't in the business of intervening in the "process of justice." The Geneva Conventions are not about justice but about good treatment. The I.C.R.C. was there to make sure that the men were decently treated and fed and that when they were released they would get some assistance to get back to their villages. Dark looks were exchanged, and there was a lot of clicking of tongues as we bowed and made our way out through the cell door.

THROUGHOUT MY TIME in Kabul, people told me I had to meet Alberto. Like all local legends, he did not seem to have a second name—just Alberto. He wasn't exactly a typical I.C.R.C. delegate, but he did seem to symbolize for many reporters what was admirable about the organization. Alberto turned out to be Alberto Cairo, a tall, thin, and intense Italian in his mid-forties with round wire-rimmed glasses, graying hair, and an air of excited distraction. He had been in Kabul for seven years—longer than any other delegate and longer than almost any other expatriate in the city. He was there when rockets landed on Kar Teh Seh hospital, and the corridors filled with the wounded and the dying; and when the refuge for the blind was damaged by explosion; and when the mujahideen terrorized the Marastoon shelter for the mentally ill; and when cholera broke out; and when a Red Cross nurse was killed southwest of the city; and when Red Cross ambulances were targeted. He had come as a physiotherapist and now ran the I.C.R.C.'s biggest prosthetic-limb program anywhere: the orthopedic center at Wazir Akbar Khan hospital. It was a thriving workshop, staffed largely by Afghan war-wounded themselves. He took me on a tour, kissing an amputee who was trimming new limbs on a lathe; ruffling the hair of another, who was shaping plaster around the stumps of recent amputees; and mock-punching the arm of a third, who was firing new casts in ovens. The heels on the artificial limbs, I learned, are cut from old Soviet tires. "The quality is excellent," Alberto said.

Many of Alberto's patients were young Afghans who, never having been to school, entered the militias because the warlords were the only people who paid a wage. Now they stumped up and down the garden paths outside, heaving their strange new limbs across the gravel. Besides the warriors, there were other, even grimmer casualties of war. In one room, a small bundle of gray-blue rags lay on a hospital cot. Alberto pulled aside its cover and revealed a dusty-faced child of about seven shivering in her sleep. "Polio," he said. Immunization programs had faltered, and, with the war, polio had returned to Afghanistan.

Alberto wanted me to meet his chief administrator, Moheb Ali, a twenty-six-year-old paraplegic in a wheelchair, who was wearing sky-blue pajamas. Two years earlier, an I.C.R.C. orthopedic center had found itself caught in the cross fire between the government guns on Television Hill and an Islamic militia holed up in a warren of streets nearby. The expatriate staff withdrew, but Moheb volunteered to remain in the center, with a radio and a few guards, to do what he could to protect the artificial limb–making machinery in case the compound should be stormed. The fighting continued for twelve days. Alberto, with the delegation in the middle of town, could communicate with Moheb only by radio, and at times the gunfire was so loud that he could barely make out what Moheb was saying. Then, one night, government forces fought their way into the compound and seized Moheb and his guards, thinking that they belonged to the militia they had been fighting. "I was saying my prayers," Moheb dryly recalled.

Alberto, desperate, persuaded a government minister to order his troops to leave Moheb alone. The next night, the militia took the orthopedic center. Helpless in his wheelchair in the bunker, Moheb heard them coming through the compound gate. "I began to pray again and read the Holy Koran," he said. This time, government artillery drove the militia out of the compound.

Two weeks later, Alberto finally got both factions to agree to let an I.C.R.C. convoy evacuate Moheb and his guards. The food had all but run out, and the batteries in Moheb's radio were almost dead. Moheb was ready. He and the guards had managed, amid continuous rocket fire, to prepare most of the machinery for evacuation. Almost single-handed, Moheb had saved the center.

For me, this was the story of Afghanistan, where two sides, so maddened by weapons and ideology, would not scruple to kill each other over possession of a Red Cross orthopedic center. For Alberto, the story explains why he has remained in Kabul. When Moheb had finished his tale, Alberto looked at me with an expressive Italian shrug and said, "How can I leave?" What Moheb thinks his story means took a minute or two to discover. He turned back to his laptop computer and his purchase orders and then said something so softly I had to ask him to repeat it: "The Red Cross made me brave."

IV

AT THE I.C.R.C. HEADQUARTERS in Geneva, I shared my puzzlement about the organization—my respect for the courage of its delegates, my sense of futility about what they were trying to do—with Gilbert Holleufer, a communications adviser, who is preparing the organization's message for the next century.

I was reared amid the antiwar politics of the sixties, and to me the organization's message seemed paradoxical, even suspect. Holleufer, a somber, thoughtful Swiss-German man with large, mournful eyes, understood the contradictions. "In modern ethics, war is inhuman, and therefore undefendable," he said. "The driving ideologies of this world are ecology, human rights, and humanitarian ethics. War is increasingly banned from modern culture." Human rights, of course, is a recent concept. The laws of war predate it by many millennia: the idea that warriors should show compassion to their victims may be a lot older than the one that all human beings have rights and should be treated as equals. Dunant's original genius lay in his acceptance of war as an essential ritual of human society, which can be tamed but will never be eradicated. And this ritual, Holleufer argues, is at odds with the essentially pacifist assumptions of our age—our culture of human rights. There are many delegates in the I.C.R.C. itself, Holleufer added, who find the organization's acceptance of war difficult to stomach. "Many Red Cross people think we have to fight for peace," he said. They believe that the I.C.R.C. should be on the side of "justice, security, and freedom." But perhaps the I.C.R.C.'s core attachment, he said, was not to these values but to a darker thought: the idea that, even amid death and fear and carnage, dignity could still prevail among warriors.

Holleufer flipped a video on. It was one that he was hoping to distribute to television stations in the former Yugoslavia. It consisted of a succession of gray line drawings of combatants patrolling ruined streets and a simple voice-over: "A warrior does not kill prisoners. A warrior does not kill children. A warrior does not rape women." The voice-over was striking for what it did not say. It did not appeal to any notion of compassion or decency. It did not appeal to anyone as a human being. It appealed solely to the combatants as warriors.

How many of us are prepared to put our moral trust in soldiers? After all, Lieutenant Calley was an officer in an army with a weighty tradition of honor, but that tradition did not stop the massacre at My Lai. My time with the I.C.R.C., however, had taught me to rethink my antiwar culture. The Red Cross acknowledges that a warrior's honor is a slender hope, but it may be all there is to separate war from savagery. And a corollary hope is that men can be trained to fight with honor. Armies train people to kill, but they also teach restraint and discipline; they channel aggression into ritual. War is redeemed only by moral rules, and, as Holleufer says, "the Red Cross is the guardian of the rules."

The problem, he concedes, is that more and more warriors no longer play by the rules. Modern technology has steadily increased the distance, both moral and geographic, between the warrior and his prey. What sense of honor can possibly link the technician who targets the Tomahawk cruise missile and the civilians of Baghdad a thousand miles away? At the other end of the scale, the global market in small arms is breaking up the modern state's monopoly on the means of violence. The disintegrating states of the world are literally flooded with junk weapons, old Kalashnikovs for the most part, which can be bought in the marketplace for the cost of a loaf of bread. With weapons this cheap, violence becomes impossible for the state to contain. The history of war has been about the state's confiscating violence from society and vesting it in a specialized warrior caste. But if the state loses control of war, as it has in so many of the world's red zones of insurgency and rebellion—if war becomes the preserve of private armies, gangsters, and paramilitaries—then the distinction between battle and barbarism may disappear.

THE BATTLE OF SOLFERINO lasted from sunrise to sunset on one day. The Angolan civil war lasted thirty years. The Afghan war has gone on since 1979. The butcheries in Rwanda and Burundi began with independence in the sixties and have been recurring ever since. In times past, war observed its own ecological limits. Conflicts burned themselves out as they used up soldiers and supplies and food. Now war is able to outrun the carrying capacity of the local ecology.

Outside humanitarian intervention may also be helping, not to contain war, but to keep it going. The I.C.R.C.'s devoted delegates struggle to enable the population to survive the unendurable, but lurking in the back of every delegate's mind is the possibility that in patching up the wounded, housing the homeless, and comforting the widows and orphans, they are simply prolonging the conflict, giving a society the capacity to keep on destroying itself. Outside intervention also encourages the formation of a new sort of moral alibi among combatants. It is a universal feature of postmodern war for combatants to appeal to outside intervention to stop the conflict; when, invariably, outside intervention fails to stop hostilities, the combatants use this as an alibi to keep on fighting. A dependency syndrome sets in—most visible in the Balkans—in which the failure of interventionists is taken as a moral excuse to keep on waging war. At the same time, the humanitarian interveners themselves become dependent on the hostilities they are trying to contain or stop. The emergence of ragged, or endemic, war at the end of the twentieth century has helped the I.C.R.C. to rapidly expand its budget and staff. To put it bluntly, war has been good for business, troublingly so, and there seems no easy way out of the vicious cycle of intervention prolonging the agonies it was supposed to stop.

The desolation of places like Afghanistan also brings home the extent to which humanitarian intervention serves as an alibi for the larger failure of the great powers to put a stop to the fighting in the first place. As long as the Red Cross is there, the outside world can at least say that "we" are fitting limbs on maimed children. Red Cross delegates themselves are bitterly aware of the extent to which their good work has helped legitimize comprehensive disengagement by outside powers.

For the larger problem, not just in Afghanistan but in most of the danger zones of the post–Cold War world, is the disintegration of states. This is a problem that humanitarian action alone cannot redress. The state's monopoly has been broken: its armories have been ransacked, and the weapons, so cheap and easy to use that a child can learn to kill in a quarter of an hour, have been diffused like a virus through the whole social tissue of poor societies.

If you have spent time in Zaire, Rwanda, Afghanistan, the former Yugoslavia, one conclusion stares you in the face. More than development, more than aid or emergency relief, more than peacekeepers, these societies need states, with professional armies under the command of trained leaders. Militias must be disarmed; weapons must be confiscated. The violence that has spread down through the sinews of the society to its very youngest and most vulnerable members, its children, must be confiscated and tamed. In the Western antiwar tradition, we are so used to thinking of the state as an agent of violence, as the instigator of war, that we forget the state's other historical role in our own development, which was to confiscate weaponry from the militias and retinues of the medieval warrior barons and to secure to a single authority the monopoly over the legitimate use of force. However paradoxical it may sound, the police and armies of the nation-state remain the only available institutions we have ever developed with the capacity to control and channel large-scale human violence. The question then becomes this: How are those of us lucky enough to live in zones of relative safety to assist those in the zones of danger to re-create viable states? How do we intervene without making things worse, either by introducing new weapons or, more subtly, by assisting populations to prolong the conflict? Sometimes, hard as it is, the best thing to do is to do nothing: to let a victor emerge and then to assist him to establish and sustain the monopoly on violence upon which order depends. In the other case, where the adversaries are too evenly balanced to allow a decisive outcome, we may have to intervene on the side that appears to be most in the right and assist it to consolidate power. This means, of course, accepting that war may be an unavoidable solution to ethnic conflict. It means accepting a moral pact with the devil of war, seeking to use its flames to burn a path to peace.

Although most Red Cross delegates would deny it, they too have made their pact with the devil of war. What the history that stretches back to Dunant seems to teach is that war survives all forms of outrage at its barbarity, that it is pointless to dream of a world beyond war or to imagine a world where the warrior's art is no longer needed, and that the path of moral reason lies in subtlety, even casuistry: accepting the inevitability, sometimes even the desirability of war, and then trying, if it is possible, to conduct it according to certain rules of honor. The struggle to make warriors obey the codes of honor is not a futile or hopeless task. Rules honored more in the breach than in the observance are still worth having. There are human and inhuman warriors, just and unjust wars, forms of killing that are necessary and forms that dishonor us all. The Red Cross has become the keeper of these distinctions; they are the sentinels between the human and the inhuman.

NEVER HAVE SENTINELS between the human and the inhuman been more necessary. Never has their work been more dangerous. On December 17, 1996, six Red Cross personnel were asleep in their beds in an I.C.R.C. hospital at Novye Atagi, near Grozny, in Chechnya. The hospital, which provided medical care for all factions in the conflict, had been officially accepted by both Russian and Chechen authorities. The hospital compound was guarded by unarmed Chechen staff. At around 4 A.M., an unknown number of armed and masked men scaled the wall of the compound. They all had pistols fitted with silencers. They knocked one guard unconscious, pumped several shots into the hospital computers, and then made their way to the dormitory block where the Red Cross staff were sleeping. The killers were questioned by a Chechen nurse, and she was told to get out of the way. The six sleepers—from Canada, Norway, New Zealand, the Netherlands, and Spain—were shot at such close range that powder burns were found on them. A male delegate who rose to meet his attacker took a bullet in the shoulder and escaped execution by feigning death. The members of the paramilitary squad took flight when one of the Chechen guards—who, against orders, was armed—fired a warning shot in the air: they scaled the wall and disappeared. None of the Chechen or Russian groups or factions have claimed responsibility for the crime. The incident was the worst massacre of Red Cross personnel in history. At a hurried meeting of heads of delegations to consider security, the I.C.R.C. acknowledged that the new, semicriminalized forms of war exposed the delegates to dangers they had never seen before. But they did not accept the necessity of posting armed guards inside hospitals, or of providing armed escorts for their convoys. They reaffirmed their faith in the legitimacy of the Red Cross emblem.

As the coffins bearing the bodies of the six staffers—Nancy Malloy, Sheryl Thayer, Hans Elkerbout, Ingeborg Foss, Gunnhild Myklebust, and Fernanda Calado—were brought out onto the tarmac at the Geneva airport, Tobias Bredland, a Norwegian Red Cross doctor who had survived the attack, stood at attention, wearing his Red Cross badge on the lapel of his winter coat. At the organization's headquarters, a flag in the courtyard stood at half-mast, and, in the room where a Christmas party was to have been held, staff and delegates gathered to listen to Cornelio Sommaruga. He had received a message from a field delegate, and he read it out:

> All our endeavor is based on the belief that, even in the middle of the worst depravities of war, man retains a fundamental minimum of humanity. Events like this can

make it very difficult to maintain this belief. But without it we would have to admit that nothing distinguishes man from beast, *and that we will not admit.*

Sommaruga pronounced the last phrase with particular emphasis. The room was hushed for several minutes. Then the men and women of the Red Cross walked silently out into the cold winter night.

The Nightmare from Which
We Are Trying to Awake

I

A DISILLUSIONED YOUNG TEACHER in a turn-of-the-century
Dublin school is struggling through a history lesson with adolescent pupils who are just as bored as he is. He asks them the name
of the ancient battle where Pyrrhus won his Pyrrhic victory, and
as they mumble the wrong answers, his mind begins to wander.
Why is history so suffocating? Is it nothing more than a lesson in
futility and folly? Is this what his pupils unconsciously know as
they yawn at their desks? Is this why they hang on the silence,
waiting for the bell to deliver them back to the noise of the play-
ground and the still unforeclosed possibilities of youth?

After his pupils flood out into the school yard, the young
teacher goes to his headmaster's study to collect his weekly wages.
Turn-of-the-century Ireland is still very much in the British

Empire, and Mr. Deasy's study is decorated with the iconography of empire and British union: a tintype of Albert Edward, Prince of Wales, and sporting prints of famous English horses. Mr. Deasy identifies with this iconography of Protestant imperial power: he baits the young teacher and calls him a Fenian, while the young teacher bites his tongue and conjures up in his mind all the savagery incarnated in the Protestant conquest: the Catholic corpses left behind by Cromwell's bloody passage through Ireland. This is history at its most suffocating: the blood-soaked myth that forecloses all benign possibilities. "Ulster will fight and Ulster will be right": Mr. Deasy intones all the adamantine slogans of resistance to home rule and Irish national independence. But there are darker myths imprisoning Mr. Deasy and his kind. He waves his finger at the young teacher. "Mark my words . . . England is in the hands of the Jews. In all the highest places: her finance, her press. . . . Old England is dying." Having dropped the coins of the young teacher's pay into his hands, Mr. Deasy makes a little joke. Why is it, he asks, that Ireland "has the honor of being the only country which never persecuted the Jews?" "Why, sir?" "Because she never let them in."

The Jews have sinned against the light, Mr. Deasy instructs him, and history—which is moving toward the manifestation of the glory of God—has proved it so.

To which Stephen Dedalus—Joyce's protagonist in *Ulysses*—famously replies: "History is a nightmare from which I am trying to awake."

History was not just the anti-Semitic philistinism and crabbed imperial arrogance of the Irish Protestant ascendancy—as deposited in the foul sediment of one turn-of-the-century schoolmaster's brain. There was a "Fenian" version to escape as well. In *A Portrait of the Artist as a Young Man*, the nationalist

Davin tells Dedalus, "Try to be one of us. In heart you are an Irishman," when Dedalus announces, "This race and this country and this life produced me. I shall express myself as I am." To Davin's protest, "A man's country comes first. Ireland first, Stevie. You can be a poet or mystic after," Dedalus replies with cold anger: "Ireland is the old sow that eats her farrow."

Joyce's writing is a long rebuke to versions of history as heritage, as roots and belonging, as comfort, refuge, and home. His was the opposite claim: You could be yourself only if you escaped home, if you struggled awake from the dreams of your ancestors. For Joyce the artist, coming awake meant finding a language of his own against the compulsion of linguistic tradition and inheritance. As he says in *Portrait of the Artist,* "when the soul of a man is born in this country there are nets flung at it to hold it back from flight. You talk to me of nationality, language, religion. I shall try to fly by those nets." And fly by them Joyce did: to Trieste, Paris, and Zurich, from *Portrait* to *Ulysses* to *Finnegans Wake,* from home to exile, from the language of his birth to a language uniquely his own. To come awake as an artist was to create something that transcended both personal and national past. To awake was to come to yourself, to force a separation between what the tribe told you to be and what you truly were.

What is nightmarish about nightmare is that it permits no saving distance between dreamer and dream. If history is nightmare, it is because past is not past. As an artist and as an Irishman, Joyce was only too aware that time in Ireland was simultaneous, not linear. In the terrible quarrel at the beginning of *Portrait* over the meaning of the Irish nationalist politician Parnell's disgrace and death, when Dante screams triumphantly, "We crushed him to death!" and Mr. Casey sobs with pain for his dead king and Stephen's father's eyes fill with tears, it is clear that Parnell's death is not in the past at all. In the quarrel, past, present, and future are ablaze together, set alight by time's livid flame.

To awake from history, then, is to recover the saving distance between past and present and to distinguish between myth and truth. Myth is a version of the past that refuses to be just the past. Myth is a narrative shaped by desire, not by truth, formed not by the facts as best we can establish them but by our longing to be reassured and consoled. Coming awake means to renounce such longings, to recover all the sharpness of the distinction between what is true and what we wish were true.

It has become common to believe that we create our identities as much as we inherit them, that belonging is elective rather than tribal, conscious rather than unconscious, chosen rather than determined. Even though we cannot chose the circumstances of our birth, we can chose which of these elements of our fate we make our defining inheritance. Artists like Joyce have helped us think of our identities as artistic creations and have urged us to believe that we too can fly free of the nets of nationality, religion, and language.

The truth is that the nets do bind most of us. Few of us can be artists of our own lives. That does not make us prisoners: we can come awake; we do not need to spend our lives in the twilight of myth and collective illusion; we can become self-conscious. Few of us will ever create as fully as Joyce the imaginative ground on which we stand or the language in which we speak. But though Joyce's hard-won freedom may be beyond most of us, his metaphor of awaking points to a possibility open to us all. In awaking, we return to ourselves. We recover the saving distance between what we are told to be and what we are. This saving distance is the space for irony. We wake: we tell our nightmare to someone; its hold on us begins to break; it begins to seem funny or at least untragic. We may still shudder in the telling, but at least we can share it. We can lighten up. The day can begin.

I I

WHAT DOES IT MEAN for a nation to come to terms with its past? Do nations have psyches the way individuals do? Can a nation's past make a people ill as we know repressed memories sometimes make individuals ill? Conversely, can a nation or contending parts of it be reconciled to its past as individuals can, by replacing myth with fact and lies with truth? Can nations "come awake" from the nightmare of their past, as Joyce believed an individual could?

In his *Introductory Lectures on Psychoanalysis* Freud once baffled his audience by remarking that there was knowing and there was knowing and they were not the same. We think we know a lot of things but we do not really know them at all. We can know something in our heads without knowing it in our guts. We can forgive people in our heads without forgiving them in our hearts. Knowledge can be propositional or dispositional. For the former to become the latter, it must be—in Freud's phrase—"worked through." A two-way process is involved: what we know in our heads must become something we know in our guts; what we know in our guts must become something we know in our heads. Psyche and soma, which have been divided by trauma, must be reunited again. The process is bound to be slow and painful. In working through death or loss, our bodies often resist what our minds know to be true; or our mind resists believing what the body already feels. To master trauma is not just to bring body and mind together in acceptance; it is also to recover, in both body and mind, a sense that the past is past. This means shifting the past out of the present; replacing psychological simultaneity with linear sequence; slowly loosening the hold of a grief or an anger whose power traps us in an unending yesterday.

Can we speak of nations "working through" a civil war or an atrocity as we speak of individuals working through a traumatic memory or event? The question is not made any easier to answer by the ways our metaphors lead us on. We tend to vest our nations with consciences, identities, and memories as if they were individuals. It is problematic enough to vest an individual with a single identity: our inner lives are like battlegrounds over which uneasy truces reign; the identity of a nation is additionally fissured by region, ethnicity, class, and education. It is not merely that each of these elements of a nation will make its own reckoning with trauma but that the real reckoning is molecular—within the conscience of the millions of individuals who compose a nation. Yet nations have a public life and a public discourse, and the molecular reckonings of individuals are decisively affected by the kinds of public discussion of the past that a nation's leaders, writers, and journalists make possible.

Questions about how nations "work through" their past are mysterious, but they are also urgent and of practical significance. In 1993, after seventy-five years of civil war, partition, terrorist insurgency, and intercommunal violence, the people of northern and southern Ireland embarked once again on an attempt to awake from their Joycean nightmare and begin a joint process of healing and reconciliation. In Nelson Mandela's South Africa, a truth commission has been touring the country attempting to provide a forum in which both victims and perpetrators can come to terms with apartheid. If the perpetrators choose truth— that is, if they disclose what they knew and what they did—they can avoid judgment and obtain amnesty and pardon. The War Crimes Tribunal in the Hague is both prosecuting crimes committed in the Balkan war and making them public in order to assist in eventual reconciliation. In the African city of Arusha, a similar tribunal is collecting evidence about the genocide in Rwanda, believing here, too, that truth, justice, and reconciliation are indissolubly linked. In all these instances—Ireland, South Africa, the Balkans, Rwanda—the rhetoric is noble but the rationale is unclear. Justice in itself is not a problematic objective, but whether the attainment of justice always contributes to reconciliation is anything but evident. Truth likewise is a good thing, but as an African proverb reminds us, truth is not always good to say.

In Archbishop Tutu's own words, the aim of his truth commission is "the promotion of national unity and reconciliation" and "the healing of a traumatized, divided, wounded, polarized people." Laudable aims, but are they coherent? Look at the assumptions he makes: that a nation has one psyche, not many; that the truth is certain, not contestable; and that, when the truth is known by all, it has the capacity to heal and reconcile. These are not so much epistemological assumptions as articles of faith about human nature: that the truth is one and, if we know it, it will make us free.

The rest of us look on and applaud, perhaps forgetting to ask how much truth our own societies can stand. All nations depend on forgetting: on forging myths of unity and identity that allow a society to forget its founding crimes, its hidden injuries and divisions, its unhealed wounds. It must be true, for nations as it is for individuals, that we can stand only so much truth. But if too much truth is divisive, the question becomes, How much is enough?

Faith in the healing virtues of truth inspired the commissions in Chile, Argentina, and Brazil that sought to find out what happened to thousands of innocent people "disappeared" by the military juntas during the 1960s and 1970s. All these commissions believed that, if the truth were known, a people made sick by terror and lies would be made well again. The results, though, were ambiguous. As Pilate asked as he washed his hands, What is truth? At the very least, it consists of factual truth and moral truth, of narratives that tell what happened and narratives that attempt to explain why it happened and who is responsible. The truth commissions in South America had more success in establishing the first than in promoting the second. They did succeed in establishing the facts about the disappearance, torture, and death of thousands of persons, and this information allowed relatives and friends the consolation of knowing how the disappeared met their fates. It says much for the human need for truth that the relatives of victims preferred the facts to the false comforts of ignorance. It also says a great deal for the moral appeal of magnanimity that so many of these people should have preferred the truth to vengeance or even justice. It was sufficient for most of them to know what happened; they did not need to punish the transgressors in order to put the past behind them.

But the truth commissions were also charged with the production of public truth and the remaking of public discourse. Their mandate was to generate a moral narrative—explaining the genesis of evil regimes and apportioning moral responsibility for the deeds committed under those governments. And here they were infinitely less successful.

The military, security, and police establishments were prepared to let the truth come out about individual cases of disappearance. Factual truth they could live with; moral truth was out of the question. They fought tenaciously against prosecutions of security personnel and against shouldering responsibility for their crimes. To have conceded ethical responsibility would have weakened their power as institutions. Such was the resistance of the military in Argentina and Chile that the elected governments that created the commissions had to choose between justice and their own survival, between prosecuting the criminals and risking a military coup or letting them go and allowing a democratic tradition to take root.

The record of the truth commissions in Latin America has disillusioned many of those who believe that shared truth is a precondition of social reconciliation. The military and police apparatus survived the inquiries of the truth commissions with their legitimacy undermined but their power intact. The societies in question used the truth commissions to foster the illusion that they had put the past behind them. Indeed, the truth commissions facilitated exactly the kind of false reconciliation with the past that they had been created to forestall. The German writer and thinker Theodor Adorno observed this false reconciliation at work in his native Germany after the war:

> "Coming to terms with the past" does not imply a serious working through of the past, the breaking of its spell through an act of clear consciousness. It suggests, rather, wishing to turn the page and, if possible, wiping it from memory. The attitude that it would be proper for everything to be forgiven and forgotten by those who were wronged is typically expressed by the party that committed the injustice.

The dangers of false reconciliation are real enough but it is possible that disillusion with the truth commissions of Latin

America goes too far. It was never the truth commissions' charge to transform the military and security apparatus any more than it is Archbishop Tutu's charge—or within his power—to do the same in South Africa. Truth is truth; it is not social or institutional reform.

Nor, when the truth is proclaimed by an official commission, is it likely to be accepted by those against whom it is directed. The police and military have their own truth—and it exerts its hold precisely because for them it is not a tissue of lies. It is unreasonable to expect those who believed they were putting down a terrorist or insurgent threat to disown this idea simply because a truth commission exposes the threat as having been without foundation. People, especially people in uniform, do not easily or readily surrender the premises upon which their lives are based. Repentance, if it ever occurs, is an individual matter. All that a truth commission can achieve is to reduce the number of lies that circulate unchallenged. In Argentina, it is now impossible to claim, for example, that the military did not throw half-dead victims into the sea from helicopters. In Chile, it is no longer permissible to assert in public that the Pinochet regime did not dispatch thousands of entirely innocent people. Truth commissions can and do change the frame of public discourse and public memory. But they cannot be judged failures because they fail to change behavior and institutions. That is not their function.

A truth commission can winnow out the facts upon which society's arguments with itself should be conducted. But it cannot bring these arguments to a conclusion. Critics of truth commissions sometimes speak as if the past were a sacred text, like the American Constitution or the Bill of Rights, that has been stolen and vandalized and that can be repaired and returned to a well-lit glass case in some grand public rotunda. But the past has none of the fixed and stable identity of a document. The past is an argument, and the function of truth commissions, like the function of honest historians, is simply to purify the argument, to narrow the range of permissible lies.

Truth commissions have the greatest chance of success in societies that already have created a powerful political consensus behind reconciliation, such as in South Africa. This consensus may have less to do with moral agreement about the need to purge the poisons of the past than with a prudential political calculation, shared by most people, that judicial vindictiveness has the potential to tear society apart and even to unleash civil or racial war. In such a context, where truth seems a less divisive objective than justice, Tutu's commission, even as it forces the disclosure of painful truth, may well reinforce the political consensus that created his commission.

In places like the former Yugoslavia, on the other hand, where the parties have murdered and tortured one another for years and where the crimes of the sons and daughters have often built upon the crimes of fathers and grandfathers, the prospects for truth, reconciliation, and justice are much bleaker. These contexts, however bleak, are instructive because they illustrate everything that is problematic in the relation between truth and reconciliation.

The idea that reconciliation depends on shared truth presumes that shared truth about the past is possible. But truth is related to identity. What you believe to be true depends, in some measure, on who you believe yourself to be. And who you believe yourself to be is mostly defined in terms of who you are not. To be a Serb is first and foremost not to be a Croat or a Muslim. If a Serb is someone who believes Croats have a historical tendency toward fascism and a Croat is someone who believes Serbs have a penchant for genocide, then to discard these myths is for both groups to give up a defining element of their own identities. The war has created communities of fear, and these communities cannot con-

ceive of sharing a common truth—and a common responsibility—with their enemies until they are less afraid, until fear of the
other ceases to be a constitutive part of who they take themselves
to be.

Obviously, identity is composed of much more than negative
images of the other. Many Croats and Serbs opposed these negative stereotypes and the nationalist madness that overtook their
countries. There were many who fought to maintain a moral
space between their personal and national identities. Yet even
such people—the human-rights activists and antiwar campaign-
ers—are now unable to conceive that one day Zagreb, Belgrade,
and Sarajevo might share a common version of the history of the
conflict. Agreement on a shared chronology of events might be
possible, though even this would be contentious; but it is impossible to imagine the three sides ever agreeing on how to apportion
responsibility. The truth that matters to people is not factual or
narrative truth but moral or interpretive truth. And this will
always be an object of dispute in the Balkans.

It is an illusion to suppose that "impartial" or "objective" outsiders would ever succeed in getting their moral and interpretive
account of the catastrophe accepted by the parties to the conflict.
The very fact of being an outsider discredits rather than rein-
forces one's legitimacy. For there is always a truth that can be
known only by those on the inside. Or if not a truth—since facts
are facts—then a moral significance to these facts that only an
insider can fully appreciate. The truth, if it is to be believed, must
be authored by those who have suffered its consequences. But the
truth of war is so painful that those who have fought each other
rarely if ever sit down to author it together.

The problem of a shared truth is also that it does not lie "in
between." It is not a compromise between two competing versions.
Either the siege of Sarajevo was a deliberate attempt to terrorize

and subvert a legitimately elected, internationally recognized state, or it was a legitimate preemptive defense by the Serbs of their homeland against Muslim attack. It cannot be both. Outside attempts to write a version of the truth that does "justice" to the truth held by both sides are unlikely to be credible to either.

Nor is an acknowledgment of shared suffering equivalent to shared truth. It is relatively easy for both sides to acknowledge each other's pain. Much more difficult—indeed, usually impossible—is shared acknowledgment of who bears the lion's share of responsibility. For if aggressors have their own defense against truth, so do victims. Peoples who believe themselves to be victims of aggression have an understandable incapacity to believe that they too have committed atrocities. Myths of innocence and victimhood are a powerful obstacle in the way of confronting responsibility, as are atrocity myths about the other side.

Hill-country Serbs in the Foca region of Bosnia told British journalists in the summer of 1992 that their ethnic militias were obliged to cleanse the area of Muslims because it was well known that Muslims crucified Serbian children and floated their bodies down the river past Serbian settlements. Since such myths do not need factual corroboration in order to reproduce themselves, they are not likely to be dispelled by the patient assembly of evidence to the contrary. A version of this particular atrocity myth used to be spread about the Jews in medieval times. The myth was not true about the Jews and it is not true about Muslims, but that is not the point. Myth is so much sustained by the inner world—by paranoia, desire, and longing—that it is dissolved, not when facts from the outer world contradict it, but only when the inner need for it ebbs away.

To speak of myths is not to dispute that one side may be more of a victim than the other or to question that atrocities happen.

What is mythic is that the atrocities are held to reveal the essential identity—the intrinsic genocidal propensity—of the peoples in whose name they were committed. All the members of the group are regarded as susceptible to that propensity even though atrocity can be committed only by specific individuals. The idea of collective guilt depends on the idea of a national psyche or racial identity. The fiction at work here is akin to the nationalist delusion that the identities of individuals are or should be subsumed into their national identities.

Ethnic war solders together individual and collective identities. Both aggressors and victims can bear only so much responsibility, as individuals, for what they have done or suffered. They need the absolution provided by collective identity.

Ethnic war isolates aggressors from the truth of their own actions. If ethnic cleansing is successful, it removes victims and leaves the victor in possession of a terrain of undisputed truth. Who, after all, is left to remind the winners that someone else once owned these houses, worshipped here, buried their dead in this ground? Ethnic cleansing eradicates the accusing truth of the past. In its wake, the past may be rewritten so that no record of the victim's presence is allowed to remain. Victory encloses the victor in a forgetting that removes the very possibility of guilt, shame, or remorse, the emotions necessary for any sustained encounter with the truth.

Victims of ethnic war, for their part, have lost the sites that validate their version of the truth. They can no longer point to their homes, their houses of worship, their graves, for those places are gone. In exile, victimhood itself becomes less and less real. The victims keep pleading for a truth to which fewer and fewer people give notice, and outsiders who tell them to face up to the truth are in essence asking them to accept the fact of their defeat.

Victims of ethnic war may refuse this truth, preferring to stick together in refugee camps and settlements rather than disperse as individuals to face the world alone. Refusing the truth of defeat is a condition of their dignity but it also traps them in an identity of collective victimhood.

And so both sides in ethnic war end up trapped in collective identities: the victors in their amnesia, the victims in their refusal to accept defeat. These fates shape memory and personality, and, over the long term, make it impossible for either side to be reconciled to the truth.

III

IF THE PROSPECTS for shared truth are grim, and the prospects for reconciliation even grimmer, what is there to be said for the prospects of justice? The vital function of justice in the dialogue between truth and reconciliation is to disaggregate individual and nation, to disassemble the fiction that nations are accountable like individuals for the crimes committed in their name. The most important task of war crimes trials is to "individualize" guilt, to relocate it from the collectivity to the individuals responsible. As Karl Jaspers said of the Nuremberg trials in 1946, "For us Germans this trial has the advantage that it distinguishes between the particular crimes of the leaders and that it does not condemn the Germans collectively."

By analogy with Nuremberg, therefore, the Hague trials are not supposed to put the Serbian, Muslim, or Croatian peoples in the dock but to separate the criminals from the nation and to lay the guilt where it belongs, on the shoulders of individuals. Yet trials inevitably fail to apportion all the guilt to all those responsible.

For one thing, small fry tend to pay the price for the crimes committed by big fish, thereby reinforcing the sense that justice is not definitive but arbitrary. For another, such trials do not necessarily break the link between individual and nation. Clearly Nuremberg failed to do so: the world still regards the Germans as being collectively responsible and, indeed, the Germans themselves still accept this responsibility. The German novelist Martin Walser once wrote that when a Frenchman or an American sees pictures of Auschwitz, "he doesn't have to think: We human beings! He can think: Those Germans! Can we think: those Nazis! I for one cannot. . . ." The most that can be said for war crimes trials is that they do something to unburden a people of the fiction of collective guilt, by helping them to transform guilt into shame. This appears to have happened in Germany, to some extent. But Nuremberg alone could not have accomplished it. As Ian Buruma points out in *The Wages of Guilt*, many Germans dismissed the Nuremberg trials as nothing more than "victor's justice." It was not Nuremberg but the strictly German war crimes trials of the 1960s that forced Germans to confront their part in the Holocaust. Verdicts reached in a German courtroom benefited from a legitimacy that the Nuremberg process never enjoyed.

Nor was coming to terms with the past just a matter of digesting the message of the domestic war crimes trials. It took a million visits to concentration camps by German schoolchildren, the publication of a thousand books, the airing of the Hollywood television series *Holocaust*—a vast reckoning between generations, which is still going on.

But such a reckoning is possible only when a publicly sponsored discourse gives it permission to happen. West Germany made a collective attempt to confront its Nazi past; as a vanquished nation occupied by the Western powers, it had no choice.

In its classrooms, in its language of public commemoration, and occasionally in its leaders' public gestures of reparation and atonement, West Germany faced up to its past and, in doing so, has gradually allowed the past to become the past.

In East Germany, on the other hand, public discourse passed the burden of the Nazi past westward, to the other side of the "anti-fascist wall"; the official fiction was that the East was the heir of the Communist antifascist resistance and therefore absolved of all responsibility for Hitler's crimes. Even though this fiction must have contradicted ordinary people's memory of their own complicity with Hitler, going along with it was convenient, and for the war criminals among them, organized public amnesia provided a refuge and an exculpation. Over time, however, the public lie became a liability for the regime: official amnesia simply confirmed the suspicion that the regime, as a whole, depended for its survival on historical mendacity. When the public arena is filled with lies, private memory remains in hiding. Indeed, in East Germany, public forgetting engendered private forgetting. But over the very long term, a regime's present-day legitimacy is inevitably undermined if it persists in telling lies about the past. The very rapidity with which East Germany collapsed suggests that the gulf between public lie and private truth had created a long-standing crisis of legitimacy. The breach in the wall brought the whole flimsy structure down. Now that the Stasi is no more, East Germans must awake to the reality that they and their parents colluded not with one dictatorship but with two, Red and Black, from 1933 until 1989.

The enormity of this double inheritance explains why East Germany since 1989 has gone through the most convulsive of all attempts to purge itself of the past: state trials, truth commissions, dismissal of secret police informers, full disclosure of secret police files. The thoroughness of the process was impressive, but its speed was suspect. It was as if the West German elite, which pushed the process through, believed that one single drastic operation could drain away the poison of the past once and for all. Perpetrators and accomplices colluded in this speedy forgiving and forgetting, and many victims did, too, simply to get on with the rest of their lives. Forgetting was made easier by the explosive invasion of the capitalist market into the East. Everyone had waited so long for the consoling bath of capitalist consumption that they could be forgiven for believing that it would cleanse them of the past as well. But the past is tenacious, simply because it holds so many clues to the present. Whenever a people ask themselves, Who are we?– as the East Germans must—they are forced to ask themselves, How did we let ourselves submit? No questions of national identity in the present can ever avoid encountering the painful secrets of the past. In this sense, as long as these questions are alive—and they are perpetually alive in Germany—there can be no forgetting.

IV

GERMANY'S ENCOUNTER with its Red and Black past was forced upon it by defeat. The Allies insisted on Nuremberg; the West Germans insisted upon de-Stasification in the East. But what happens when societies are *not* forced, by defeat, to face up to the accusing truth of the past? What happens when there are no truth commissions, no war crimes trials? Until the 1980s, Soviet Russia did not—and could not—face up to the crimes of Stalinism. Here official culture actively repressed the collective past because public knowledge of the regime's crimes would undermine whatever legitimacy the regime still retained from its successful defeat of the Nazis. Indeed, the historical mythology of the great patriotic war—of the great victory against fascism—made it extremely difficult for the society to confront the forms of Red fascism that flourished in its midst. Those who fought for the preservation of memory—Solzhenitsyn, Sakharov, Pasternak, and Akhmatova—were persecuted not simply because they demanded rights of free expression but because they spoke a truth about the regime's past that, if publicly known, would have destroyed Soviet legitimacy altogether. This truth—that the regime survived by extermination—was known to millions; hence millions had to be terrorized or killed to maintain the regime's fictions. As early as the mid-1950s, the men of Khrushchev's generation—who had only barely survived the Terror—began admitting that the cost of maintaining a regime based on historical lies was becoming prohibitive. And as a new generation—the men who came to power under Gorbachev—slowly worked their way up the hierarchy, they carried with them the stories of terror and extermination whispered to them by their parents. The increasingly flagrant contradiction between the public lies they were obliged to tell and their own private or family memories of Stalinist repression ended by undermining the Gorbachev elite's determination to hold on to power. The contradiction sowed deep doubt about the moral legitimacy of socialism in the very soul of an elite that was simultaneously confronting economic stagnation and social decomposition. As in East Germany, reconciliation with the past was possible only with the demolition of the system itself, and, as in East Germany, the collapse came very suddenly, as if the edifice had long before developed cracks in its foundation and was awaiting only a final blow from historical events.

But if the will to power of the members of the Gorbachev elite was sapped by the contradiction between their own family memories and mendacious public myth, the same was not true of many millions of ordinary party members. They felt no such contradiction or doubt. Russian society as a whole has never been de-Stalinized. There have been no truth commissions or public trials, and the party's acknowledgment of its guilty past, for example in Khrushchev's speech to the party congress in 1956, occurred only when the facts were too well known to be denied any longer. Indeed, the torturers have been decorated, promoted, and retired with honor. There have been no trials of the executioners of the Lubyanka or the camp commandants of Magadan. Thanks to Solzhenitsyn, there has been some truth about the past, but there has been no justice and hence there cannot be any reconciliation between the two Russias, between the majority who went along with the regime and the minor-ity—whose numbers run into the millions—who were sent to the gulag. The awakening to truth remains confined to a small liberal minority of the old Gorbachev elite and the educated middle and professional classes in the big cities. For countless former party members, there is nothing to repent, nothing to apologize for. In the absence of justice, then, even the truth can be denied.

The case of contemporary Russia indicates that it is not enough to have *some* truth about the past. No matter how mag-nificent the efforts of Solzhenitsyn and the heroic research of people like Vitaly Shentalinsky, who forced the KGB to give up the secrets of its persecutions of Russian writers, the mere disclosure of truth—of a record of unpunished crime—does not allow the closure, the resolution that judicial trials can force a resisting society to accept.

Justice may be essential, then, but it is best to be modest about what trials can achieve. The great virtue of legal proceedings is that rules of evidence establish otherwise contestable facts. In this sense, war crimes trials make it more difficult for societies to take refuge in denial. But if trials assist the process of uncovering the truth, it is doubtful whether they assist the process of reconciliation. The purgative function of justice tends to operate on the victims' side only. While victims may feel justice has been done, the community from which the perpetrators come may feel that they have been made scapegoats. All one can say is that leaving war crimes unpunished is worse: the cycle of impunity remains unbroken, societies remain free to indulge their fantasies of denial.

V

IT IS OPEN TO QUESTION whether justice or truth actually heals. It is an article of faith with us that knowledge, particularly self-knowledge, is a condition of psychic health, yet every society, including ours, manages to function with only the most precarious purchase on the truth of its own past. Every society has a substantial psychological investment in its heroes. To discover that its heroes were guilty of war crimes is to admit that the identities they defended were themselves tarnished. Which is why a society is often so reluctant to surrender its own to war crimes tribunals, why it is so vehemently "in denial" about facts evident to everyone outside the society. War crimes challenge collective moral identities, and when these identities are threatened, denial is actually a defense of everything one holds dear.

There are many forms of denial, ranging from outright refusal to accept facts as facts to complex strategies of relativization.

In these, one accepts the facts but argues that the enemy was equally culpable or that the accusing party is also to blame or that such "excesses" are regrettable necessities in time of war. To relativize is to have it both ways: to admit the facts while denying full responsibility for them.

Resistance to historical truth is a function of group identity: nations and peoples weave their sense of themselves into narcissistic narratives that strenuously resist correction. Similarly, regimes depend for their legitimacy on historical myths that are armored against the truth. The legitimacy of Tito's regime in Yugoslavia depended on the myth that his partisans led a movement of national resistance against the German and Italian occupations. In reality the partisans fought fellow Yugoslavs as much as they fought the occupiers and even made deals with the Germans to strengthen their hand against domestic opponents. Since these facts were common knowledge to any Yugoslav of that generation, the myth of brotherhood and unity required the constant reinforcement of propaganda.

The myth of brotherhood and unity may have been pointing toward a future beyond ethnic hatred, but by lying about the past, the regime perpetuated the hatreds it was trying to get Yugoslavs to overcome. By repressing the real history of the interethnic carnage between 1941 and 1945, the Titoist regime guaranteed that such carnage would return. Competing versions of historical truth—Serb, Croat, and Muslim—that had no peaceful, democratic means of making themselves heard in Tito's Yugoslavia took to the battlefield to make their truths prevail. The result of five years of war is that a shared truth is now inconceivable. In the conditions of ethnic separation that characterize all the major successor republics to Tito's Yugoslavia, a shared truth—and hence a path from truth to reconciliation—is barred, not just by hatreds but by institutions too undemocratic to allow counter-vailing truth to circulate.

It is not undermining the war crimes tribunal process to maintain that the message of its truth is unlikely to penetrate the authoritarian successor states of the former Yugoslavia. The point is merely that one must keep justice separate from reconciliation. Justice is justice, and within the strict limits of what is possible, it should be done. Justice will also serve the interests of truth. But the truth will not necessarily be believed, and it is putting too much faith in truth to believe that it can heal.

When it comes to healing, one is faced with the most mysteri-ous process of all. For what seems apparent in the former Yugoslavia, in Rwanda, and in South Africa is that the past con-tinues to torment because it is *not* past. These places are not liv-ing in a serial order of time but in a simultaneous one, in which the past and the present are a continuous, agglutinated mass of fantasies, distortions, myths, and lies. Reporters in the Balkan war often discovered, when they were told atrocity stories, that they were uncertain whether these stories had occurred yesterday or in 1941 or 1841 or 1441. For the tellers of the tales, yesterday and today were the same. Simultaneity, it would seem, is the dream time of vengeance. Crimes can never be safely fixed in the histor-ical past; they remain locked in the eternal present, crying out for blood. Joyce understood that in Ireland the bodies of the past were never safely dead and buried; they were always roaming through the sleep of the living in search of retribution.

Nations, properly speaking, cannot be reconciled to other nations as individuals can be to individuals. Nonetheless, individ-uals are helped to heal and to reconcile by public rituals of atone-ment. When President Alwyn of Chile appeared on television to apologize to the victims of Pinochet's crimes of repression, he created the public climate in which a thousand acts of private repentance and apology became possible. He also symbolically cleansed the Chilean state of its association with these crimes. German Chancellor Willy Brandt's gesture of going down on his knees at a death camp had a similarly cathartic effect by officially associating the German state with the process of atonement.

These acts contrast strikingly with the behavior of the political figures responsible for the war in the Balkans. If, instead of writing books niggling about the numbers exterminated at Jasenovac, President Tudjman of Croatia had gone to the site of the most notorious of the Croatian extermination camps and publicly apologized for the crimes committed by the Croatian Ustashe against Serbs, Gypsies, Jews, and Communist partisans, he would have liberated the Croatian present from the hold of the Ustashe past. He would also have dramatically increased the chances of the Serbian minority's accepting the legitimacy of an independent Croatian state. Had he confronted the past, the war of 1991 might have been prevented. He chose not to, of course: despite having been an anti-Ustashe partisan himself, he depended, in his campaign for independence, on support, both financial and moral, from former Ustashe in exile. Moreover it proved impossible, both for Tudjman and for much of his electorate, to admit Croatia's historical responsibility for war crimes, since it was central to the very rationale behind the drive to independence that Croats were historical victims of the aggrandizing Serbs. Nonetheless, it remains true that a gesture of atonement on Tudjman's part would have purged Croatia of its legacy of genocide; it would have invited Croatians to replace self-pity and hysterical denial of the past with conscientious discourse, and it would have sent an unmistakable message of fraternity to the Serbs, perhaps preventing them from surrendering, with equal self-pity and hysteria, to the Serbian myth that Serbs can be safe only inside a Greater Serbia. Societies and nations are not like individuals, but their leaders can have an enormous impact on the mysterious process by which individuals come to terms with the painfulness of their societies' past. Leaders give their societies permission to say the unsayable, to think the unthinkable, to rise to gestures of reconciliation that people, individually, cannot imagine. In the Balkans, not a single leader had the courage to exorcise his nation's ruling fantasies.

The chief moral obstacle in the path of reconciliation is the desire for revenge. Now, revenge is commonly regarded as a low and unworthy emotion, and because it is regarded as such, its deep moral hold on people is rarely understood. But revenge—morally considered—is a desire to keep faith with the dead, to honor their memory by taking up their cause where they left off. Revenge keeps faith between generations; the violence it engenders is a ritual form of respect for the community's dead—therein lies its legitimacy. Reconciliation is difficult precisely because it must compete with the powerful alternative morality of violence. Political terror is tenacious because it is an ethical practice. It is a cult of the dead, a dire and absolute expression of respect.

When nations or communities fight each other, they are often only continuing a conflict initiated generations earlier. What did or didn't happen at Drogheda, what Cromwell did or didn't do on his conquering passage through Ireland in the civil war—these are the obstacles that continue to stand in the path of reconciliation in the Ireland of the 1990s. Time and again, the slaughter inflicted by one side in Bosnia in 1992 was repaying a slaughter in 1942. This cycle of intergenerational recrimination has no logical end. Sons cannot—in any meaningful sense—pay their fathers' debts or avenge their fathers' wrongs. But it is the very impossibility of intergenerational vengeance that locks communities into the compulsion to repeat. As in nightmare, each side hurls itself at the locked door of the past, seeking in vain to force it open.

Intergenerational conflict can be pacified only when both sides make elementary distinctions between guilt and responsibility. Sons are not guilty for their fathers' crimes and no peace will come until they stop feeling responsible for avenging the wrongs their fathers suffered. They do remain responsible for telling the truth about them. They must admit what was done. But they must also commit themselves to avoiding the repaying of like with like.

Reconciliation means breaking the spiral of intergenerational vengeance. It means substituting the vicious downward spiral of violence with the virtuous upward spiral of mutually reinforcing respect. Reconciliation can stop the cycle of vengeance only if it can equal vengeance as a form of respect for the dead. What each side, in the aftermath of a civil war, essentially demands is that "the other side" face up to the deaths it caused. To deny the reality of these deaths is to treat them as a dream, as a nightmare. Without an apology, without recognition of what happened, the past cannot return to its place as the past. The ghosts will continue to stalk the battlements. Of course, an apology must reflect acceptance of the other side's grief, something deeper than the Englishman Haynes's well-meaning but offhand remark in *Ulysses:* "An Irishman must think like that, I daresay. We feel in England that we have treated you rather unfairly. It seems history is to blame."

Joyce's great rebellion was against the idea of history as fate, compelling each generation to reproduce the hatreds of the previous one because keeping faith with the dead—honoring their memory—seems to require taking up arms to avenge them. Reconciliation built on mutual apology accepts that history is not fate, that history is not to blame. Nor are cultures or traditions— only specific individuals whom history must name. This last dimension of reconciliation—the mourning of the dead—is where the desire for peace must vanquish the longing for revenge. Reconciliation has no chance against vengeance unless it respects the emotions that sustain vengeance, unless it can replace the respect entailed in vengeance with rituals in which communities once at war learn to mourn their dead together. Reconciliation must reach into the shared inheritance of the democracy of death to teach the drastic nullity of all struggles that end in killing, the unending futility of all attempts to avenge those who are no more. For it is an elementary certainty that killing will not bring the dead back to life. This is an inheritance that can be shared, and when it is shared there can be that deep knowing that sometimes comes when one wakes from a dream.

Notes on Sources

Is Nothing Sacred? The Ethics of Television

On the Ethiopian famine of 1984 and the charitable response in Britain, I am indebted to assistance from the public relations department of Oxfam; for a study of television coverage of the famine, see William Boot, "Ethiopia: Feasting on Famine," *Columbia Journalism Review,* March-April 1985, pp. 47–49; on the background to the famine, see Fred Halliday and Maxine Molyneux, *The Ethiopian Revolution* (1983); Graham Hancock, *Ethiopia: The Challenge of Hunger* (1985); and Ryszard Kapuscinski's brilliant portrait of the Ethiopian monarchy in decay, *The Emperor* (1983). On the origins of the idea of natural law in sixteenth- and seventeenth-century Europe, see Richard Tuck, *Natural Rights Theories* (1979); Quentin Skinner, *The Foundations of Modern Political Thought* (1978); and Peter Stein, *Legal Evolution* (1981). On the doctrine of toleration, see Henry Kamen, *The Rise of Toleration* (1967); John Locke, *A Letter Concerning Toleration* (1990); Richard Popkin, *The History of Scepticism* (1979); and Michael Walzer, *On Tol-*

eration (1997); on the liberal idea of putting cruelty first among the vices, see Judith Shklar, *Ordinary Vices* (1984). See also my own *The Needs of Strangers* (1985). On the slave trade and its abolition, see David B. Davis, *The Problem of Slavery in the Age of Revolution* (1975); for a detailed discussion of the Christian debate on the ethics of charity in times of famine and its impact on European thought, see Istvan Hont and Michael Ignatieff (eds.), *Wealth and Virtue: The Shaping of Political Economy in the Scottish Enlightenment* (1983). For a modern discussion of the ethical dimensions of famine and famine relief, see Amartya Sen, *Poverty and Famines* (1981); the Marxist critique of bourgeois universalism is in Lucio Colletti (ed.), *Marx: Early Writings* (1975); see also M. Merleau-Ponty, *Humanisme et Terreur* (1972); the Roland Barthes essay is to be found in his *Mythologies* (1973). I am also indebted to Susan Sontag, *On Photography* (1978), and to John Berger, *About Looking* (1980). The quotation from Don McCullin is taken from "A Life in Photographs," *Granta*, Winter 1985; on television and its traditions and forms of narrative, I am indebted to the work of Anthony Smith, especially *The Shadow in the Cave* (1973), and *From Books to Bytes* (1995). On the idea of the sacred, see Marcel Gauchet, *Le désenchantement du monde* (1985); Regis Debray, *Critique of Political Reason* (1983); and above all, Leszek Kolakowski, *Religion* (1983).

The Narcissism of Minor Difference

Despite having made Samuel Huntington's *The Clash of Civilizations* (1996) a bête noir throughout this chapter, I believe it is only fair to point out that his emphasis on the cultural and religious roots of ethnic antagonism is a welcome relief from the functionalist and "realist" mode of American foreign policy analysis. On the Yugoslav catastrophe, I owe a debt to Laura Silber and Allan Little, *The Death of Yugoslavia* (1995); Misha Glenny, *The Fall of Yugoslavia* (1992); and the essays by Steven Pavlovitch and others in Jacques Rupnik (ed.), *De Sarajevo à Sarajevo* (1992). My own journeys through the war zones of Croatia in 1993 are detailed in my *Blood and Belonging: Journeys into the New Nationalism*

(1993); on national identity, I learned from Anthony Smith, *National Identity* (1991); Benedict Anderson, *Imagined Communities* (1983); Ernest Gellner, *Nations and Nationalism* (1983); Eric Hobsbawm, *Nations and Nationalism since 1870* (1990); and Elie Kedourie, *Nationalism* (1960). On the transition to democracy in Eastern Europe, I learned particularly from Timothy Garton Ash, *The Uses of Adversity* (1991); on the Cain myth, I am particularly indebted to Regina M. Schwartz, *The Curse of Cain* (1997); on autism, see Hans Magnus Enzensberger, *Civil War* (1994). Freud's references to narcissism and minor difference are to be found in "The Taboo of Virginity" (1917), in *Freud on Sexuality* (Pelican Freud Library, vol. 7), p. 272; "Group Psychology and the Analysis of the Ego" (1921), in *Freud* (Pelican Freud Library, vol. 12), p. 131; and in *Civilization and Its Discontents* (1929), also in Pelican Freud Library, vol. 12, p. 305. On race and difference, I wish to acknowledge K. Anthony Appiah and Amy Gutmann, *Color Conscious* (1996), and Kenan Malik, *The Meaning of Race* (1996). Finally, I am indebted to the audiences who have listened to this argument as it developed: at the inaugural lecture, Pavis Centre, Open University (1994); the Morrell Lecture on Toleration, University of York (1994); and Parks Lecture on Toleration, University of Southampton (1995).

The Seductiveness of Moral Disgust

In thinking about the new internationalism of the early 1990s, I learned much from David Rieff's excellent article "Whose Internationalism, Whose Isolationism" in *World Policy Journal,* no. 2, Summer 1996, and from his *Slaughterhouse: Bosnia and the Failure of the West* (1995). I am also indebted to the articles in the special issue of *Social Research,* vol. 62, no. 1, Spring 1995, on *Rescue: The Paradoxes of Virtue,* edited by Arien Mack. Joseph Conrad's connection to the Congo, and possible sources for the figure of Kurtz, have been discussed in an excellent article by Adam Hochschild, "Mr. Kurtz, I Presume," in *The New Yorker,* April 14, 1997; for the Rwandan genocide, I want to acknowledge the work of Philip Gourevitch in *The New Yorker,* especially "The Return," January

20, 1997. On *le droit d'intervention humanitaire,* see Bernard Kouchner, *Le Malheur des autres* (1992); for a critique of humanitarianism, see Alain Finkielkraut, *L'Humanité perdue* (1996); on the chaos narrative, see Robert D. Kaplan, *The Ends of the Earth* (1996).

The Warrior's Honor

On the Red Cross, the Geneva Conventions, and the laws of war, I am indebted to François Bugnion, *Le comité international de la croix rouge et la protection des victimes de la guerre* (1994); I also consulted the annual reports of the I.C.R.C., 1990–1996, together with selected issues of its journal, *The International Review of the Red Cross.* On the Red Cross in action between 1936 and 1945, see Marcel Junod, *Warrior without Weapons* (1982); on the I.C.R.C. in the Gulf War, see Christophe Girod, *Tempête sur le Désert* (1995). For a view of the Red Cross that insists that its unspoken mission is ending war, not merely controlling it, see N. O. Berry, *War and the Red Cross* (1997); on the Red Cross in Yugoslavia, see M. Mercier, *Crimes without Punishments* (1994); Roy Gutman, *Witness to Genocide* (1993); Jan Willem Honig and Norbert Both, *Srebrenica* (1996). On Afghanistan, I benefited from Barnett R. Rubin, *The Search for Peace in Afghanistan* (1995), and from discussions with Fred Halliday, professor of international relations at the London School of Economics. The best available treatment of the history of the laws of war is in the collection edited by Michael Howard, George J. Andreopoulous, and Mark R. Shulman, *The Laws of War: Constraints on Warfare in the Western World* (1994). Finally, on the transformation of modern war, see John Keegan, *A History of Warfare* (1993), together with his incomparable study, *The Face of Battle* (1977). See also Martin Van Creveld, *The Transformation of War* (1991); Leroy Thompson, *Ragged War* (1994); Robert D. Kaplan, *The Ends of the Earth* (1996); P. Delmas, *The Rosy Future of War* (1997); and C. H. Gray, *Postmodern War* (1997). I am especially indebted, finally, to Eric Hobsbawm's "Barbarism: A User's Guide" in his *On History* (1997).

The Nightmare from Which We Are Trying to Awake

In thinking about German war guilt, I owe a debt of gratitude to Ian Buruma, *The Wages of Guilt* (1991). Timothy Garton Ash, *The File* (1997), is essential reading on the subject of East Germany's working-through of its Communist past and its network of Stasi informers. On Gorbachev's Russia and the role of memories of Stalinism in undermining the self-confidence of the elite, see David Remnick's account in *Lenin's Tomb* (1993); see also Vitaly Shentalinsky, *Arrested Voices: Resurrecting the Disappeared Voices of the Soviet Regime* (1995). The special edition of *Index on Censorship*, vol. 25, no. 5, 1996, on *Wounded Nations, Broken Lives: Truth Commissions and War Tribunals,* contains an excellent article by Alberto Manguel on the Argentina Truth Commission. Ariel Dorfman's play *Death and the Maiden* is the most penetrating account of the issues of justice, revenge, and forgiving in the Chilean context. The best overview of truth commissions and the punishment of state crimes is Stanley Cohen's "State Crimes of Previous Regimes: Knowledge, Accountability and the Policing of the Past," in *Law and Social Inquiry,* vol. 20, no. 1, 1995. I also learned much from Avishai Margalit's published lecture "To Remember, to Forget, to Forgive," delivered at the Nexus Institute, Tilburg, Netherlands, in May 1996. Theodor Adorno's "What Does Coming to Terms with the Past Mean?" is in his *Gesammelte Schriften,* vol. 10, pt. 2, pp. 555–572 (1977); translation by Timothy Bahti and Geoffrey Hartman. I have discussed Jasenovac and the Croatian relationship to its Ustashe past in my *Blood and Belonging: Journeys into the New Nationalism* (1993). See also Slavenka Drakulic, *Balkan Express* (1993); Misha Glenny, *The Fall of Yugoslavia* (1993); and Alain Finkielkraut, *Comment peut-on être croate* (1992). On national identity, see Anthony D. Smith's *National Identity* (1991). Finally, my discussion of Ireland and Irish nationalism owes much to Roy Foster, *Modern Ireland* (1988), and also his *Paddy and Mr. Punch* (1993). On Joyce, I benefited from Emer Nolan, *James Joyce and Nationalism* (1995), and James Fairhall, *James Joyce and the Question of History* (1993).

Index

About the Author

Writer, historian, and television producer MICHAEL IGNATIEFF was born in 1947 in Toronto. He holds a Ph.D. from Harvard and has taught at Cambridge, Oxford, the Ecole des Hautes Etudes in Paris, and the University of California at Berkeley. His book on ethnic nationalism in the 1990s, *Blood and Belonging*, won Canada's highest literary award, the Governor-General's Prize, and was the basis of the acclaimed television series. A frequent contributor to *The New Yorker*, *The New York Review of Books*, and the *New Republic*, he is also the author of a memoir, *The Russian Album*, which won Britain's Heinemann Award; a study of altruism, *The Needs of Strangers;* a book on the penitentiary in the industrial revolution, *A Just Measure of Pain;* and a novel, *Scar Tissue*, which was short-listed for the Booker Prize in 1993. He is currently working on the first authorized biography of Isaiah Berlin and on a history of the moral imagination in the twentieth century, which will also be produced for television. Both works are forthcoming from Metropolitan Books. Michael Ignatieff now lives in London.